INSIGHTS

PETER HAVERTY

authorHOUSE

AuthorHouse™ UK
1663 Liberty Drive
Bloomington, IN 47403 USA
www.authorhouse.co.uk
Phone: UK TFN: 0800 0148641 (Toll Free inside the UK)
UK Local: 02036 956322 (+44 20 3695 6322 from outside the UK)

© 2020 Peter Haverty. All rights reserved.

No part of this book may be reproduced, stored in a retrieval system, or transmitted by any means without the written permission of the author.

Published by AuthorHouse 10/28/2020

ISBN: 978-1-6655-8095-3 (sc)
ISBN: 978-1-6655-8096-0 (e)

Library of Congress Control Number: 2020919971

Print information available on the last page.

Any people depicted in stock imagery provided by Getty Images are models, and such images are being used for illustrative purposes only.
Certain stock imagery © Getty Images.

Scriptures marked RSV are taken from the REVISED STANDARD VERSION (RSV): Scripture taken from the REVISED STANDARD VERSION, Grand Rapids: Zondervan, 1971.

This book is printed on acid-free paper.

Because of the dynamic nature of the Internet, any web addresses or links contained in this book may have changed since publication and may no longer be valid. The views expressed in this work are solely those of the author and do not necessarily reflect the views of the publisher, and the publisher hereby disclaims any responsibility for them.

I would like to acknowledge and thank Frs Robert Farrell and Andrew Soane for their helpful advice along with Mrs Anne Marie Walker and the formattin by Miss Judith Sheehan.

CONTENTS

Introduction ix
Nature xi
Grace xiii
Original Sin xv
Transcendental Order xvii

PART 1

Chapter 1: God 1

Paragraphs 1-10 There are no agnostics. Apostasy. God's Attributes. Everlasting Love. The Incarnation. Goodness. Sacramental Words. The Devil's Sin. The Cause of the Fall: Bishop Challoner.

Chapter 2: Jesus Christ 10

Paragraphs 11- 20 The human predicament, Transfer, Incarnation, Redemption, Charity, Sacred Heart, the Cross, Transcendental love, Cross and suffering, drop of Blood.

Chapter 3: Christianity 21

Paragraphs 21 -30 Our Lord with His Death has shown us how to die. Sins against the Holy Spirit. Obstinacy in sin. Final impenitence. Spiritual envy. Transcending the Abyss. Sharing. Interior life. Holy Spirit. The insight of power.

PART II

First Step: Creation and Fall 37
The Devil's Temptation of Eve 41
Consequences of the Fall 43
Effect of the Consequences of Original Sin 46
God's Plan of Redemption 48
The Narrow Gate 51
Divine Filiation 55
Hope of Becoming Saints 58
Sin and Lukewarmness 62
Confession 67
The Last Things 71
Death 73
Judgment 78
Purgatory 83
Hell 88
Heaven 94
The Incarnation 98
The Birth of Our Lord 109
The Hidden Life 114
Public Life 122

The Last Supper: The New Commandment 133
The Passion and Death of Our Lord Jesus Christ 141
The Glorious Resurrection of Our Lord Jesus Christ 151
The Ascension of Our Lord and the Coming of the Holy Spirit 157

INTRODUCTION

WHEN I FIRST THOUGHT OF writing a little book on Christianity, the idea I had in mind was something along the lines of Isaac Asimov's *'Words of Science'*, but then I began to realise that on the one hand this would be very boring to read, and on the other difficult, if not impossible, to understand without some sort of philosophical introduction. Now, although I am starting out with a philosophical and theological introduction, it is intended to be just that, an introduction, but an introduction to make the rest of the **insights** understandable.

And what do I mean by **insights**? Well, many years ago, sitting in a library, I said to myself 'wouldn't it be wonderful if I had all the knowledge contained in all these books in my head?' As the years rolled by and I had studied a certain number of books, I began to realise what a lot of copying was going on. Everybody just copied what the others before them had said and in fact each one contributed very few **insights** of their own, and furthermore, the ideas they themselves had contributed were rather poor. I began to realise that there were relatively few really worthwhile **insights**. Now, like everything else, one has one's favourites and I realise that the ones I am presenting here may not be yours. Nevertheless, if what I have seen as profound inspirations are not your cup of tea, they may encourage you to compile your own list.

Another point has to be made and it is the point that Scheeben, the German Theologian, made in his *'Mysteries of Christianity'*, i.e. that the Christian teaching is composed of mysteries because it concerns supernatural things and therefore, we cannot fully understand them.

This does not mean to say we cannot have some inkling of what they are about. These **insights**, then, are meant to be just that - some kind of **insight** into Christian mysteries.

Some basic principles to begin with:

<u>Nature, Grace, Original Sin and the Transcendental Order</u>

NATURE

IN PHILOSOPHICAL THINKING YOU WILL not get very far unless you understand what is meant by **Nature.**

Everything we know about this earth has a nature of some sort. It is the philosophical principle that makes a thing to be what it is, with its characteristic qualities. Nature is the essence of a thing. But nature adds something to the notion of essence; it means essence inasmuch as the source of activities.

Perhaps some examples may help. The old philosophy teachers used to ask their pupils: 'What is it that makes a horse, a horse'? And then answer: 'Why *horseness* of course'! A horse neighs, gallops, eats hay and all sorts of other things. It is its nature to do so. Then there are lots of other things it cannot do, like writing home to mother, saying he is sorry for kicking. A horse does not laugh or cry.

Contrary to what the evolutionists believe, and bear in mind that it is just a question of belief, God has given everything its nature. The vast majority of animals can see. Some insects have hundreds of eyes. Man has just two, situated at the front of his face so, although we do have peripheral vision, we can see only what lies ahead. Horses, however, have two eyes, one on each side of the head, like most shy and vulnerable animals (antelopes, deer etc) which are often preyed upon, so that they can see behind them and then run away when danger looms. Lions and tigers and other animals which prey on others, need not fear what comes from the rear and have their eyes at the front. Does this tell us something about humans? Anyway, the main point I want to make is that we will say that it is man's nature to see. And so, anyone who is blind, is deprived of something natural.

It was St Augustine who pointed out that privation is what we call **evil**. The notion of evil for him, was to be lacking in something natural, that is, what belongs to that thing by nature, or, in other words, what God intended it to have.

Being able to see does not define man's nature, since he shares it with pretty well all other animals. So, how do you define a nature? This was one of Aristotle's concerns. As a scientist he realised that, especially in the animal world they had their animality in common with all the rest and then they had something special to them; the specific difference that made them into a species all their own.

What sets a man apart from the rest, giving us the human species, is his ability to reason, to work things out using his intelligence. So, we can say: <u>man is a rational animal</u>.

Now it is being able to define what man is in his nature or essence, that is - being rational, that gives us the basis of ethics or moral science. You go to an art school to become an artist - a man or woman who is better at drawing and painting. You go to a School of Engineering or a College of Technology to become a better technician or engineer – a person whose ability with machines is superior. So, what do you go to an ethics school for? Why to be a better <u>person</u> of course. Now, in order to be a <u>better</u> person, you need to know what 'man' is essentially. Now since man is a <u>rational</u> animal, he has to learn in the School of Ethics what principles he needs and then apply them so as to perform <u>actions</u> which are rational and lead himself to <u>become more rational</u>. This is why we need education.

GRACE

IN THEOLOGICAL THINKING YOU WILL not get very far unless you understand what is meant by **Grace**.

When God created man, he endowed him with sanctifying grace. This is a theological term meaning a quality which likens man to God. It signifies friendship with God, and is a certain participation in the divine life. The word 'grace' has Latin roots and signifies something freely given and also beautiful. In old English we speak of a 'gradely lass', meaning handsome, or good-looking. As free, therefore, grace is a gratuitous gift from God and the first man - Adam - was given this gift by God. In Genesis we read: *'and God created man to his own image and likeness'(Gen 1:27)*. This is a sentence of both <u>fact</u> and of <u>intent</u>. It describes what man already is, coming from God's hands, so-to-speak, and what God wants man to be.

Now, we have to be clear about this, because it is defined doctrine that the first man was endowed with what are called preternatural gifts; immortality, impassibility, integrity, and above all supernatural grace. But when the first man disobeyed God he lost God's friendship and **grace**. But since grace is gratuitous, we cannot call it privation in the strict sense. Likewise, we cannot call the consequence of the loss of grace in Adam's successors **sin**. Nevertheless, when Adam sinned through disobedience, the grace he should have bequeathed to his offspring throughout the successive generations, was withheld. Now this deprivation we call **Original Sin** even though Adam's successors are without guilt. But, remember, that is all original sin is: absence of sanctifying grace. But what are we missing? What is this sanctifying grace? Given that it is supernatural we cannot really understand it.

However, we can use a simple analogy: <u>grace is to the soul what the soul is to the body - its principle of life.</u>

When we walk through the woods and are about to step on a twig and we find it moves - it is a frog or a snake - we shout 'it's alive'. The principle of its living activities and what gives that living thing its unity is its soul. The word for soul in Latin is *'anima'* and so we speak of inanimate things and living things; those with a soul and those without. In man, this soul is the source or principle of the spiritual actions as well as the physical actions; it is the principle of unity. This is attested in a court of law. If the accused admits that it was his fist which struck the fatal blow, he cannot say <u>he</u> had nothing to do with it as if he were detached from his fist; the person and the fist are one. This is important in all moral actions, namely, the connection between the person and his faculties. Here, once more, we can speak of the importance of sanctifying grace, because, just as the soul is the source of human actions, so the soul in grace enables the human being to perform supernatural actions.

Theology teaches that only supernatural actions, that is, those performed by man in a state of grace, are meritorious for eternal life. It is as if God does not recognise actions which are not supernatural. So, when a man performs actions in a state of grace, this puts him, so-to-speak, on a par with Jesus Christ, and God from Heaven, says once more, as He said when Jesus was baptised in the Jordan, *'This is my beloved Son in whom I am well pleased'* (Mt 3:17). It is the objective then of every Christian - to perform these actions in a state of grace so that they are pleasing to God. Of course, there are other conditions to be fulfilled to qualify for being actions totally pleasing to God; but the main condition is fulfilled.

ORIGINAL SIN

YOU COULD SAY WE HAVE already spoken about original sin. This is partly true. We have said what it is *essentially*, but not what people generally think about it. In Catholic circles if someone does something wrong, people often say, 'that's because of original sin', in much the same way as people from a Protestant background might suggest it was because they were destined to act in that way, or others say it was the Devil who put them up to it. Catholics say it was original sin because they confuse the sin with its consequences. When man offended God not only was his relationship with God fractured - sin - but his own nature was wounded.

An analogy from elementary physics can help. Spread some iron filings on a white sheet of paper and put a magnet underneath the paper. On tapping the sheet, the iron filings arrange themselves along the lines of magnetic force -polarisation. Take the magnet away and tap the sheet again and you will find that all the iron filings will go higgledy-piggledy again – disorder. This is what happened when man offended God, his internal order was disrupted and he lost his <u>integrity</u>. His body and soul which, previously, were working in perfect harmony, were henceforth at loggerheads. Furthermore, this disintegration of the body parts would end up in total corruption – death, and so man lost his <u>immortality</u>. Finally, all man's faculties would deteriorate and suffer pain, so man lost his <u>impassibility</u>.

TRANSCENDENTAL ORDER

THE TRANSCENDENTAL ORDER IS THE opposite of the predicamental order. Loosely speaking, these two orders correspond to the <u>uncreated</u> order of God and the <u>created</u> order respectively. But let's go step by step. Whenever I predicate something of another, I am implicitly drawing attention to its limitation. So, for example, if I say 'Peter is a…. dog'. Until I commit myself to equating dog to Peter, Peter could be any number of things … a parrot, or a human being.

Consequently, the operation of predication clamps down on Peter and restricts this subject to just one thing… a dog. Now dogs are generally nice things, provided they don't bite. Lots of people have them as pets, but the minute I predicate dog of Peter, that's Peter finished (finite) and he cannot be anything else. Take another example…. 'Which dress shall I wear tonight? My blue dress'. Very well, blue is a beautiful colour, but by the very act of choosing the blue one, all the other dresses, red, yellow, brown etc. are eliminated. This is because all the things belong to the predicamental order. So how do I transcend it? <u>Reduplication.</u>

If I say, 'Peter is a man', this is true. I can also say 'My dress is blue', this is true; 'the weather is fine', is also true, then all these statements are true and participate in the truth.

Plato is the philosopher we have to thank for the concept of participation, although he may have got it from Socrates. We know that instead of concentrating his attention on material things and the material composition of the universe, Plato paid attention to virtues. He observed this man was truthful and this other man was truthful. And the same thing applied to goodness. This man was good and this man and this other man. All participating in the truth and goodness, but then I think this notion of participation rather went to his head because Plato decided that all the qualities of things on earth participated in a corresponding supreme idea in the *World of Ideas*. This exaggeration was a mistake. Not the basic principle, but the discovery that there were two different orders: the predicamental order, and the one that transcends it: the transcendental order. The latter, of course, is confined to just a certain number of true transcendental properties: Being, One, True, Good, and Thing. But we must call a halt to this philosophy lesson, at least for the time being, in the hope that enough has been said to appreciate the corresponding **insights**.

PART 1

CHAPTER 1

GOD

1. THERE ARE NO AGNOSTICS

EVERYBODY BELIEVES IN GOD. IT is just that some people worship and obey a God 'out there' that is, a transcendental God (Christians, Jews and Muslims), and the rest a God who is identified with the universe, or part of it; in other words, a predicamental God. But what about me, I hear you cry, 'I am an atheist'! An atheist is someone who hates God; well, obviously, you have to believe in God first before you can hate him! But what about pantheists? Well, I have just mentioned those; they are the ones like modern scientists who consider the world *is* God; that is to say self-existing or, what is the same, self-causing which, of course, is contradictory. Why then do they deny the existence of a transcendental God? <u>Because a predicamental god is much easier to manipulate</u>. They worship at the shrine of their own selfish pleasures and interests. They are idolaters. That is why God condemns them in the Old Testament. But let us go back to the scientists just for a moment so as to see a little bit better where they go wrong. In his book, *'Theology and Sanity'*, Frank Sheed says: *'We have thus caught some glimpse of why the created universe exists. That must always be the primary question. Until we know why a thing exists, we cannot properly know anything else about it. Whatever details we can discover by studying it, our interpretation of the details must always be governed by our understanding of why the thing exists at all. If we are wrong about that, the details we do know are as likely to mislead us as not. But if 'why'? is the primary question and its* answer the key to all knowledge, there are other questions to be answered in due order. The question 'why'? is followed by the question 'how'? The universe exists because God loved the very idea of it. But how did the universe come into existence? This, of course, is not at all the same as the scientist's question about the origin of the universe. Science always starts with something in existence, and its efforts to explain the origin of that something simply mean looking for some earlier something of the same created order. This study is of immense value, but our present inquiry undercuts it. Quite simply we are asking 'how is it that anything is here at all'?. When philosophers and theologians ask why anything exists, the alternative they have in mind is nothing. There might have been nothing, why is there something? This is a question which quite properly science does not ask. If in his backward progress from cause to earlier cause the scientist suddenly found himself faced with nothing, he would be inexpressibly startled. Neither his instruments nor his scientific methods are made to cope with nothing. If he found nothing in his series, he would have to call upon philosophy and theology'.

Apart from these words of wisdom from Mr Sheed, it would be useful to add that whenever Christian philosophers come up with the idea of God, they almost all come out with the question: but who caused God?, thereby showing that they have missed the point yet again: God is simply causeless; He has no cause, much less does He cause Himself. As we say in philosophy, He is <u>Pure Act</u> with no <u>Potency</u> whatsoever. So, He cannot change or be moved and it is the fact of being pure act that enables Him to cause everything else.

2. APOSTASY - AN **INSIGHT** FROM ST JOSEMARÍA ESCRIVÁ.

St Josemaría was very apostolic: very many of the points in *The Way* and his other works show this. Being a thinker, he was also very aware of human nature and human weaknesses and the attitudes and tendencies of the average unbeliever who tries to justify his avoidance of God and all He stands for.

In 1961, I was amongst a group of people in the garden of a centre of Opus Dei called Villa Tevere, which is situated near the Zoological Gardens in Rome, and I asked St Josemaría a question. 'Father', I said, 'tell us how to go about doing apostolate with people who do not believe in God'. He answered, as usual very rapidly, '*your brothers in England will be able to tell you better than I*' (or words to that effect). This answer was, of course, prompted by his humility. I found over the course of the years that he had a very shrewd assessment of how people adduce all sorts of reasons (excuses) for not believing in God. Some, as we have seen above, take the scientific route and persist in claiming for the universe an ability to sustain itself; others will say: how can there be a God who allows babies to born without arms and legs, (that is what was said during the Thalidomide crisis, when many pregnant women (particularly nurses) took this drug to avoid the morning sickness). Many more still cry out against the existence of God whenever some natural disaster occurs. This is the most ancient of all the theories that dispose of God: the problem of evil. Until St Augustine, I think I am right in saying, dualism was the answer given: there had to be two Gods one to account for evil in the world, the other to account for the good (historically, a very explicit exposé of this was given by Zoroaster). When St Augustine explained that evil was simply privation of good, the problem was solved for anyone honest enough to learn.

Unfortunately, dualism got a grip on men's minds in the form of Gnosticism and it has, as we know, done untold damage and spawned lots of other heresies.

However, to get back to the **insight** of St Josemaría. He said '*Marxism is the most ingenious idea yet devised by man to justify apostasy*'. What a marvellous **insight**! There was I trying my best to explain to students how Hegel was to blame all along, and how he had passed on the accursed seed of dialectical materialism to Feuerbach and Engels and so to Marx. Of course, it has its explanation in the historical evolution of ideas. But the real reason is that it is the Devil's work, providing mankind yet again with an excuse for keeping out of God's way.

The trouble with Marxism is that although it pretends to solve the social problem of poverty; the oppression of the poor by the rich; it just enables another set of individuals to lord it over the rest and the motivation is, as it so often is, greed. But even this is not the real reason as we can see by the result: a whole generation of people whose only concept of goodness consists in striving to be good <u>citizens,</u> instead of good men and women. This follows from the concept that the State is God. Then, of course, you get some disastrous consequences from this, that the powers-that-be are dismissive of people whose contribution is less than useful: invalids, ballet-dancers, writers etc.

3. GOD'S ATTRIBUTES, THE **INSIGHT** OF HIS UNITY

In order to understand God, we distinguish his attributes, truth, goodness, holiness, justice, mercy etc. It is very important to realise that in God they are all **one**. For this reason, it is not surprising that some Christian philosophers have made God's oneness or unity his essential attribute. However, the reason I make this preliminary observation is to understand the following **insight:**

Goodness is united in God to omnipotence; this is a truth often repeated in the prayers of the holy liturgy: 'Lord! Thou art good and all-powerful.' *'As long as the soul is not well convinced of this union of goodness and power in God, it has only half-strength, half-love, an imperfect idea of the divine succour, from which we should expect all things.'* (Père De Ravignan).

In the Apostle's Creed we say: I believe in God the Father Almighty. This means not just that God is both a Father to us and also Almighty, but that His Fatherliness is Almighty. He loves us with an almighty love!

4. EVERLASTING LOVE

Consider the eternal love which God has borne towards you; for already, long before Jesus Christ had suffered for you on the cross as man, His divine Majesty destined you to life and loved you infinitely. But when did He begin to love you? When He began to be God. And when did He begin to be God? Never. He has always been, without beginning and without end; and thus He has always loved you, and it is from all eternity that His love prepared for you the graces and favours which He has given you. He says by the prophet: *'I have loved thee with an everlasting love, and I have mercifully drawn thee to me'* (Jer. 31:3). This is another instance of the combination of attributes: in this case, eternity and love. (cf. St Francis de Sales, *'Consoling Thoughts on God and Providence'*, Chapter 2).

5. THE INCARNATION

According to St Augustine, the Incarnation is the reason for our creation. He argues that having foreseen Man's disobedience and sin, thereby deserving eternal death and condemning his offspring to the same fate, it is inconceivable in a just God, to create human beings simply to condemn them to Hell. Therefore, He created us in view of the future merits and Redemption worked by Christ. The Dogmatic Constitution on the Church no. 2: *'The plan of the eternal Father's wisdom and goodness is utterly free; it is his secret: he created the whole world, decided to raise men to a share in the divine life. He did not abandon them, when, in Adam, they fell, for he has continually offered them help to salvation, in view of Christ, the Redeemer who is the true likeness of the God we cannot see; his is that first birth which precedes every act of creation (Col 1:15). All those the Father chose before time began, who from the first were known to him, he has destined from the first to be moulded into the image of his Son, who is thus to become the eldest-born among many brethren'* (Rom 8:29). This notion is also evident in St Paul's Epistle to the Ephesians: *'He has chosen us out, in Christ, before the foundation of the world to be saints, to be blameless in his sight, for love of him; marking us out beforehand to be his adopted children through Jesus Christ'*(Eph 1:4).

6. GOODNESS IS DIFFUSIVE

The idea of the Neo-Platonists was that the whole of creation emanated from God. To explain this, Plotinus said goodness was diffusive of itself (*bonum diffusivum sui est*), which St Thomas lighted upon and made his own, leaving the rest behind. This is a remarkable philosophical insight. For when philosophers try to explain what the 'good' is they say *'id quod omnes appetunt'*, (*'that which all desire'*); then, when they explain what the will is, they say the faculty which desires the good! This is really cheating, and so the only really good explanation of what goodness is comes from Plotinus Not only is this an **insight** into what goodness is, but it also helps us very much to understand something about God, and about ourselves or rather what we should aspire to. So, for example, if you say you want to be good, this is the same as saying I want to be generous. There will be more about this later. For the moment, just try to dwell on the idea of being good and giving more!

7. SACRAMENTAL WORDS

God makes things happen without undergoing any change. As the Scholastics would say, no change from potency to act. This is what St James says in his Epistle: *'with God there is no change, or any shadow of a change'* (*'Apud Deum non est mutatio nec vicissitudinis adumbratio'*) *Jas 1:17)*. So, God just speaks, expresses a desire and things happen. This is a complete mystery to us and is another example of the difference between God's order – transcendental - and our order of things - predicamental. However, in theology we do participate in divine power in the confection of the Holy Sacraments. The theologians allow priests of the New Law to utter **sacramental words**, such as *'I baptize you'*, *'This is my body'* etc., where the priest utters a few words and something divine takes place: we are cleansed from our sins, and the bread becomes the Body of Christ. Garrigou-Lagrange has made an interesting application of this idea. He says that when Jesus was on the Cross and said to His Mother *'Behold your son' (Jn 19:26-27)*, His words, like Sacramental words, produced in Our Lady's heart a great love and tenderness towards us and we became her children. This he says was the origin of devotion to Our Lady in the Church.

8. THE DEVIL'S SIN

This power that we speak of as belonging to God alone, where He just says something and something happens, does take place in a certain sense in living persons like the Angels and men. So, for example, if I say within myself 'I am going to stand up', or 'walk away', my internal faculties obey me and it happens. So then, we see how a mere desire is translated into some sort of activity. The difference between us creatures and God is that that is just about as far as it goes; we cannot make anything else move by just willing it to happen. Well then one morning, we might say, the Devil woke up and said to himself, 'I may not be the Lord of the Universe but at least I am master of myself'! And with that seceded from God's kingdom and said within himself 'I will determine myself what will make me happy without any reference to God'. At the beginning, man was content to follow God's ordinances, but on being tempted by the Devil, he also seceded and decided that he knew better than God what was good for himself. But the truth is the opposite. God made us and knows us better than we know ourselves and above all knows what is best for us. In fact, He loves us more than we love ourselves. In the Christian religion we speak of the importance of Faith. What is Faith? Faith is to believe that God loves us more than we love ourselves; knows best what is best for us and what will make us happy. Faith then leads to obedience.

9. THE CAUSE OF THE FALL. ST JOHN OF AVILA

Given that man was in a state of grace at the beginning, and therefore that his will and intellect were in pristine condition, one may well ask 'how could man be so stupid and allow himself to be deceived by the Devil'? This is not so difficult to understand when you think that the Devil himself was more stupid and you have to bear in mind that before he fell, he was the highest in the order of the Cherubim, that is, the most intelligent of all the angels and therefore the cleverest of all God's creatures, and so it is not so surprising that he managed to deceive man. Now we, Adam's children, having being disinherited and wounded by our father Adam's sin, have a better excuse for falling. However, to make this briefer, St John of Avila tells us that it was ingratitude which caused our downfall:

> 'How was the world lost? Let us learn the answer to that, because it may perhaps show us the road to salvation. 'Homo, cum in honore esset, non intellexit, comparatus est iumentis insipientibus, et similes factus est illis' (Psalm 48, 21). ('But man when he was in honour did not understand'). Man did not value what he possessed. He wanted to rise higher, and because what he desired was beyond his reach, he lost the privileges he already had and destroyed himself. Not only did he lose God, abandoning Him for his own interests, but he lost his humanity. He who is in sin is less than a man. He is lost, <u>made like to senseless beasts,</u> since he renounced grace and was disobedient to God. (St John of Avila, 'The Holy Spirit Within'.)

I think this is a useful **insight** – it is a wonderful lesson for us, now that we have been redeemed and given grace once more; bought at a great price. Let us not be foolish like our father Adam and throw the grace which has been restored and won for us by Our Lord's great Sacrifice. Above all let us make sure we are grateful. Pope Pius XII once said that gratitude was the virtue most pleasing to God.

10. THE FALL. BISHOP CHALLONER.

In his book of Meditations, Bishop Challoner gives us his opinion of how Adam fell into sin as we read in Genesis 3:5, for, commenting on this passage, Bishop Challoner says:

> 'Man fell originally from God by proud <u>affectation</u> of superior and more excellent knowledge than God was pleased to allow him, and which might make him like to

God' (Bishop Challoner, *'Meditations for every day in the year'*, *Friday after Low Sunday*).

The question is - to what did this knowledge refer? To me this must refer to man's happiness which is the principal object of man's knowledge. He thought he knew best what would make him happy; he thought he knew better than God. But no! God knows us better than we know ourselves and knows best what will make us happy. In the Church we are continually being exhorted to have faith. What is it to have faith? To believe? What is this? The answer is that we must believe that God loves us better than we love ourselves and furthermore, knows best what will make us happy. This has the simple consequence that we must love God's will. And this brings us back to the original fall of man into sin. Under the Devil's influence he thought he knew better than God what would make him happy and lost his faith in God.

When Our Lord came on earth, He continually urged his disciples to have faith. He wanted them to believe in Him; He wanted to restore them to the belief that He had their interest at heart. His Life, Sufferings and Death are so many proofs of this. Our Lord is saying to us: 'Does all this not convince you that I love you more than you love or even could love yourself'? The net result is that not only must we love God more than self but believe in God more than self.

CHAPTER 2

JESUS CHRIST

11. THE HUMAN PREDICAMENT

EARLIER ON WE DREW A distinction between the predicamental order of created things and the transcendental order of God. On becoming man, God so-to-speak left the transcendental order and entered the predicamental order. He was born at a certain time (note that time or *quando* is one of the predicaments); lived in a certain place (this is the predicament *ubi*) and in general became subject to all human vicissitudes. Now this is interesting because we know that God's purpose in becoming man was to save all mankind from sin, and yet now He is caught in the human predicament. So, while becoming man enables God to suffer and to die and so perform the supreme sacrifice which redeems us, at the same time it confines Him to the human predicament; it limits His scope and accessibility. '*He has come so that all men might be saved*', as St Paul says to Timothy *(1 Tim 2:4)*. And yet the very means to save us, suffering in His human nature and offering Himself as a holocaust to His heavenly Father makes it practically impossible to reach the very people He wants to save: the whole human race. This is why Christ established His Church and the Holy Eucharist. On the day of Pentecost, the Holy Spirit came down on the Apostles and filled them with a great zeal for the salvation of souls. He assisted them and all their successors with the ability to recall the teaching of Jesus Christ. Then, as we know, Our Lord established the great Sacrament of the Holy Eucharist to sustain the Church in her Life of Love. It is in this way that Christ's Life is perpetuated in the disciples of Christ throughout the ages. We belong to the human predicament; we have no choice in the matter. The mere fact of being created situates us in the human predicament. But think of Christ. He chose to become Man and so enter our predicament. It is not uncommon to hear people protesting and crying out in their travails: O why was I born? Why did I come into this world? What are they doing?

They are protesting about being caught in the human predicament. It is a cry to be released; to enter the transcendental order. Or, is it perhaps just a protest against God's Will? Now when Jesus Christ became Incarnate, He entered the predicamental order of His own free will; He knew just what He was doing, knew that He would have to suffer and to die and in general have a very hard time. And yet: '...*when Christ came into the world, he said, 'Sacrifices and offerings thou hast not desired, but a body hast thou prepared for me'. Then I said, 'Lo, I have come to do thy will, O God, as it is written of me in the roll of the book"* (Heb 10:5). In other words, He came into the world happily and embraced our life, including the condition of the human predicament. This contains a lesson for us. We have to follow Christ's example and embrace the life God has given us, in spite of the fact that we had no choice in the matter. If someone says 'I did not ask to be born', it stands to reason they were powerless to do so because at that time they did not exist. The decision that we should be born was God's decision. Only Christ could say 'I want to be born' because of course He pre-existed His own birth. So, we have to take hold of our own life with both hands and say to God: 'Behold I come to do your Will just as Christ did'.

12. TRANSFER FROM THE PREDICAMENTAL ORDER TO THE TRANSCENDENTAL ORDER

In the parable of Dives and Lazarus, when Dives, the rich man asks for a drop of water, he is told that there is no passing from one side to the other. This, in philosophical terms, means there is no passing from the predicamental order to the transcendental order. Now we have already seen that when God became Incarnate, He passed from the transcendental order to the predicamental order. But that was on earth. In the case of Dives and Lazarus, the abyss is between Hell and Heaven and furthermore, we are talking of moving in the opposite direction, that is from the predicamental to the transcendental order. Now, at the present moment I do not propose to enter into the complicated problem of the communication between Hell and Heaven. I just want to draw attention to the difficulty of movement between the two orders. How, in fact, does man pass from his present state, confined as he is to the predicamental order, to the transcendental order of God in Heaven? This, of course, is precisely what Jesus Christ Our Lord came on earth to do. '*It was from the Father I came out and now I am on the way to the Father...*'*(John 16:28).* And He also said, '*I am the Way, the Truth and the Life...no-one can come to the Father except through Me...*' *(Jn 14:6).* The short answer is that we have to hang on to His coat-tails. Theologically, however, we have to put on the magic cloak belonging to Harry Potter, but instead of making us invisible, it makes us <u>transferable</u>. St Paul says: '*induimini Jesum Christum*', which translated means '*put on the Lord Jesus Christ*' *(Rom 13:14)*, and in theological terms 'be identified with Christ through <u>sanctifying grace</u>'. There are other conditions too, but this is the principal one. That is why I said at the beginning that it was important to understand the meaning of **grace**. Frank Sheed in his little book '*Theology for Beginners*', says that when a person comes to die, there is one question to ask; is this person in a state of grace or not. If the answer is yes, to Heaven he can go, but if the answer is no, he cannot go to Heaven, because he does not have the power to live there!

13. THE INCARNATION

The **insight** here is given to us by the Gospel itself. In chapter 22 of St Matthew we have the parable of the wedding feast. What wedding is this? Who is getting married? It is the union between the Second Person of the Blessed Trinity and the human race: between God and man! Those invited are members of the human race who are called to the wedding, that is, to appreciate this most extraordinary and wonderful of all God's actions: to unite Himself to the human race. Those persons who do not appreciate what God has done for them make God very angry just as the father in the parable was very angry. But He does not give up on us and insists on bringing in as many guests as will fill up the places. What about the man who was found not to be wearing a wedding garment? He represents all those members of the Church who are not in a state of grace (see above). All those who refuse to come to the wedding are those souls who by the mere fact of refusing to acknowledge Jesus Christ are already judged. Those who are like the man without a proper wedding garment will be judged on judgment day. In any case, the outcome is the same: they are bound hand and foot and cast into the outer darkness. Now I am sure we all feel that the poor little man who was seemingly too poor to buy a wedding garment was hard done by. But no, these garments were provided at the door, which means that it is possible for everybody to be in a state of grace: that is what the Sacrament of Penance is for. This is another proof that if anyone is condemned, it is not so much the sins he has committed deserving of the Second Death, but that he would not take the trouble to get out of his state of sinfulness and be sorry. It is the sin against the Holy Spirit of obstinacy in sin.

14. THE REDEMPTION

Talking to a couple of priests some years ago about the Redemption, they believed that this was accomplished by Our Lord's death on the Cross, but just that. Now this is of a piece with Protestantism. For Protestants, once you have been baptized, that's it, you are saved. For a Catholic your pilgrimage of grace has just begun, you have to perform lots of good works in a state of grace and offered to God through the Holy Sacrifice of the Mass. In the Mass just after the Consecration we have the <u>Anamnesis</u> which is the Church's obedience to those words pronounced by Our Lord at the Last Supper *'Do this for a commemoration of me'* (Lk 22:19). We do not just remember Our Lord's Death, but also His glorious Resurrection and Ascension into Heaven. What we have to remember is that God crossed over from the transcendental order to the predicamental order, but we have to accompany Him back to the transcendental order. This not only demands believing in the Resurrection of Christ and His Ascension into Heaven, but also rising again with Christ and putting on His merits, living a life of love; that is, loving in a supernatural way by means of the supernatural virtue of charity and then ascending with Him into Heaven. According to Don Francisco Luna *'Love never takes time off'*, in other words, it is eternal and so 'transcends' time. Either we love all the time or we simply do not love at all.

15. THE VIRTUE OF CHARITY

'You are to love one another as I have loved you' (John 13:34-35). These words of Our Lord at the Last Supper recorded by St John tell us, among other things, that love cannot be the same as grace. For while there can be some sort of continuity or sameness between Our Lord's love and ours, He cannot be said to be in a state of grace, for He is the cause of it. Besides, grace is a quality pertaining to man, although supernatural. But we have more evidence of this distinction between grace and charity: the parable of the wise and foolish virgins. Quite often commentators speak of the oil in the lamps as charity, and indeed it does seem as though that is the best interpretation. But when the foolish ones ask the wise ones for some of their oil, the wise ones refuse. So where is the charity there? The answer is that the oil is grace not charity, and this is incommunicable; it is necessary for the foolish ones to go to those that sell, in other words to the priests who dispense grace by way of the sacraments. But if we go back to the words of Our Lord: *'love one another as I have loved you'*; I feel sure that the Apostles looked at one another in dismay: how could they possibly love like Jesus. Now they would be looking at this in a human way: they could not even match Our Lord's human love; but if they had been fully aware that Jesus was God, they would have realized that what He was asking was absolutely impossible to them. From this we conclude that charity, which is to love with the same kind of love with which God loves us, is an infused virtue. Something which we can only obtain by asking for it from the Sacred Heart.

16. THE SACRED HEART

In the Catholic Church the great symbol of the love of Christ is the Sacred Heart: the devotion introduced by St Margaret Mary Alacoque, although others had it before her. Now the priest who did most to spread the devotion was her confessor St Claude de la Colombière. He only spoke to her about three times but was the only one to believe that her visions and revelations were from God. At any rate, this Jesuit priest really understood the message as the following quotation taken from one of his letters shows:

> 'The love of Our Lord's Heart was in no way diminished by the treason of Judas, the flight of the apostles and the persecution of his enemies. Jesus was only grieved at the harm they did themselves; his sufferings helped to assuage his grief because he saw in them a remedy for the sins committed by his enemies. The Sacred Heart was full of the most tender love; there was no bitterness in it; neither the cruelty nor the injustice he received moved it to feelings other than those of compassion and affection. I turned to Mary and asked her to obtain for me the grace to imitate Our Lord's Heart. I saw how perfectly her heart copied His: she loved those who put her Son to death and offered him to God the Father for them. This enkindled a very great love of virtue in my heart. O Sacred Hearts of Jesus and Mary truly worthy of reigning over men and angels, you shall be my models; I will try to copy you. May my heart live always in the Hearts of Jesus and Mary, and may their hearts live in mine, so that I may never do anything that is not in accordance with them.' (Claude de la Colombière *Retreat Notes*).

17. THE CROSS

Christ suffered and died for each one of us. In St Paul's Epistle to the Galatians, we read: '...*my real life is the faith I have in the Son of God, who loved me, and gave himself for me' (Gal 2:20)*. According to St John Chrysostom, when St Paul said those words he had the idea in his head that if he, Paul, had been the only one in the world who corresponded to the love of Christ, Jesus would have died just the same, and therefore, since Paul knew himself to be the very worst sinner in the world, Our Lord had died for each one as if each one of us had been the only soul in the world. This view is shared by other Fathers of the Church. Now in case anyone should query this interpretation, especially the aspect of St Paul's low opinion of himself, then I think he should read St Paul's words in his letter to Titus: *'We, after all, were once like the rest of them, reckless, rebellious, the dupes of error; enslaved to a strange medley of desires and appetites, our lives full of meanness and of envy, hateful, and hating one another. Then the kindness of God, our Saviour, dawned on us, his great love for man. He saved us; and it was not thanks to anything we had done for our own justification. In accordance with his own merciful design he saved us, with the cleansing power which gives us new birth, and restores our nature through the Holy Spirit, shed on us in abundant measure through our Saviour, Jesus Christ' (Titus 3:4-5)*.

18. CHRIST'S TRANSCENDENT LOVE

This leads us on to a further **insight** concerning Christ's transcendent love for each one of us. If it is true that He has died for each one of us, then it is also true that He lived on earth for each one of us and everything He did on earth He did for you and me. St Alphonsus said *'When you read the Passion of Christ, say to yourself as you go through the scenes of Our Lord's sufferings: He did this all for me'*! (St Alphonsus, *Meditations on the Passion of Our Lord*). This is similar to something which St Josemaría used to say. He said that when Jesus said anything to anybody in the Gospel, his words transcended the particular individual he was addressing and so he was saying it all to you…to each one of us. Of course, we find this quite difficult to grasp because we are so self-centred. I remember once, many years ago in a bus in Manchester, I was sitting behind two elderly ladies who were talking to each other. One said, as the bus passed by Owen's Park, a big block of student accommodation, 'My son has just finished his studies at school and got very good marks and is ready to go to University'. Then, when she paused for breath, the other lady got her spoke in and said 'Well my daughter is already in the University and is studying …..' we do not know what, because she had to pause for breath and the first lady continued talking about the academic achievements of *her* offspring. It did not take me long to realize that neither one nor the other was actually listening to what the other had to say. In fact, the only person who was, was me! So, you see we find it very difficult to communicate with others and find it correspondingly difficult to grasp the fact that God both speaks to each one of us and furthermore, listens to each one of us.

All this has a very useful application. When we are reading the holy Gospel we have to realize that if we put ourselves in the place of the various persons we find there and make an act of faith to believe in Jesus Christ who is addressing a particular character, then rest assured that he is addressing us, just as if we had been that character. When, for example, Jesus reproached His Disciples in the Agony in the Garden and said

'How can you sleep'? 'Could you not watch one hour with Me?' we can see that he was reproaching me also and asking me to pray. Very many people say 'I find prayer very hard, I say things to Our Lord, but He never speaks to me'. Well, in the light of the above statement we should realize that He has already said everything He wants to say to us; it is just that we do not read the Gospel with sufficient faith. *'Heaven and earth may pass away but My words will never pass away (Matt 24:35)'.* If we enter into the Gospel scenes with faith, we will find that the words of Our Lord will enter deep into our soul and show us what we should do.

19. THE CROSS AND HUMAN SUFFERINGS

Going back to Our Lord's suffering on the Cross we know that here we have the solution to this great mystery. A great many people know in general that in the Cross we have the answer to why we have to suffer. We know that the troubles in the world and all the diseases and disasters which afflict the human race are all because of that original sin of our first parents. We know that Our Lord suffered and died to make everything better and restore everything to what it had been; 'Behold I make all things new' (Rev 21:5). But the question is, how do we come to terms with the day-to-day troubles and trials of life? Here, once more, we have a beautiful and consoling **insight** from St Augustine. In a commentary on Psalm 62 St Augustine says of Our Lord: *'All that He suffered we suffered with Him, and all that we suffer, He Himself suffers in us'*. It is not just that Christ suffered *pro nobis*, but that He suffers at this present moment *in nobis*. Everyone is aware that Our Lord died for us on the Cross - but what they are not aware of is that here and now in this present moment Our Lord is suffering in us. When writing to the Colossians, St Paul says: *'I am glad of my sufferings on your behalf, as in this mortal frame of mine, I help to pay off the debt which the afflictions of Christ still leave to be paid for the sake of His body, the Church'* (Col 1:24). At the same time as this teaching of St Augustine is immensely consoling to a person who is suffering, because it means that that person is very close to Christ, it also solves quite a difficult theological problem in that we say Christ's sacrifice was enough and more than enough to wipe away the sins of the whole world and then in the next breath say with St Paul how our suffering helps to pay off the debt which the afflictions of Christ still leave to be paid. The answer is that Christ continues to pay off the debt of sin, even though He has ascended into Heaven. This also explains that very curious phrase in one of the Prefaces of the Liturgy: *semper vivit occisus* (He always lives as slain!)

20. ONE DROP OF HIS BLOOD

In the penultimate verse of the hymn, *Adoro te devote* composed by St Thomas Aquinas, we read: *'Cuius una stilla salvum facere totum mundum quit ab omni scelere'*. *('One drop of whose blood was sufficient to save the whole world and take away all its sins')*. Whether this connection is true or not, St Alphonsus appears to pick up on it and conjures up a most remarkable **insight** concerning the Priesthood and the Holy Eucharist. I found this quotation in the book called <u>Selva</u> which is a compilation of St Alphonsus's sayings for the benefit of priests, as follows: *'It was not* *necessary for the Redeemer to die in order to save the world, a drop of His Blood, a single tear, or a prayer, having an infinite value, was sufficient for the salvation of all. But to institute the priesthood, the death of Jesus Christ was necessary. Had He not died, where should we find the Victim that the priest of the New Law now offers?'*

Before I finish this passage, I must point out of course that we are speaking about the objective redemption when saying one drop of Christ's Blood is sufficient and that when Our Lord suffered all that it was possible for a man to suffer. He did this primarily to convince us how much He has loved us. God's love for us is infinite - that is in the transcendental order, but the equivalent in the predicamental order is to show this love through suffering and death.

21. THE HOLY EUCHARIST

Here is another **insight** which comes from St Peter Eymard the Founder of the Blessed Sacrament Fathers. It is, as one would expect, about the Holy Eucharist. It seems to fit in here quite nicely following the two previous paragraphs. I think it is self-explanatory, so I will content myself with just giving the quotation:

> 'Holy Communion not only gives to the sacramental Jesus the opportunity to satisfy His love; it gives Him a new life which He will consecrate to the glory of His Father...
>
> Something divine will then come to pass in the one who communicates; man will labour, and Jesus will give the grace of labour; man will keep the merit, but to Jesus will be the glory; Jesus will be able to say to His Father: 'I love Thee, I adore Thee, and I still suffer, living anew in My members.' (Notice how well this agrees with St Paul and St Augustine). This is what gives Communion its highest power: it is a second and perpetual incarnation of Jesus Christ; between Jesus Christ and man it forms a union of life and love; in a word, it is a second life for Jesus Christ.' (Peter Eymard, *Holy Communion*)

From all this we can deduce that Our Lord continues His Work of Redemption through the members of His Mystical Body, the Church. It also explains how St Peter Eymard is able to say: *'All our works must converge towards Communion as towards their end and flow from it as from the source'.* (Peter Eymard, *Holy Communion*) St Josemaría expressed the same though slightly differently when he said the Mass should be the centre and root of the interior life. This idea is repeated in the documents of the Second Vatican Council four or five times, in different documents.

CHAPTER 3

CHRISTIANITY: HOW TO LIVE AND HOW TO DIE

IN WHAT FOLLOWS I AM going to deal with those two fundamental things Jesus Christ has taught us, namely: how to live and how to die. I know very well that this is the chronological order, that is to say, we live and then we die. However, logically the order is the reverse. In order to live well, the first thing we have to consider is our death and what happens when we die. This focus on death is not a morbid obsession; it is simply practical. In order to live a good life, we have to make sure we are going in the right direction: Heaven. If we don't get to Heaven then nothing, but absolutely nothing we do on earth is of any value whatsoever. Here I repeat what I said earlier on from Frank Sheed, that there is just one question we must ask when someone comes to die: is he in a state of grace or not? For if he is then to Heaven he can go because he has the power to live there, if he is not in a state of grace then he will spend eternity in Hell! Not a pleasant thought. But once more, as I think I said before, being in a state of grace is not enough. I think the following **insights** will show this and I will deal with those relating to death first.

21. WITH HIS DEATH OUR LORD HAS SHOWN US HOW TO DIE

Many years ago, I was coming back from a funeral I had been attending and I called in at a Church. Guess what! There was another funeral Mass being celebrated! I arrived for the readings and then the priest started his homily. I will never forget the main point he made in his sermon. He said that death was a sad event, but one we had to come to terms with. This is where Our Lord helps. Jesus died, he reminded us, but He did not need to die. He died because he wanted to die. On the one hand to enable us to live forever, and on the other to show us how to die, with dignity and with peace.

22. SINS AGAINST THE HOLY SPIRIT.

There are six sins against the Holy Spirit:

1. Presumption 2. Despair 3. Resisting the known truth. 4. Envy of another's spiritual good. 5. Obstinacy in sin. 6. Final Impenitence. The first two are quite easy to understand. They both represent a challenge to God. The presumptuous man is challenging God to perform a special miracle by providing him with unmerited grace. The person who despairs is saying my sins are too much for your mercy. St Thomas says that of the two the second is worse because it represents a challenge against God's Mercy rather than His Justice and since His Mercy is a more dignified attribute, the sin constitutes a greater insult. Resisting the known truth is given to us in the Gospel of St John, where he tells us: *'When God sent His Son into the world, it was not to reject the world, but so that the world might find salvation through Him. For the man who believes in him, there is no rejection, the man who does not believe is already rejected; he has not found faith in the name of God's only-begotten Son. Rejection lies in this, that when the light came into the world men preferred darkness to light; preferred it, because their doings were evil. Anyone who acts shamefully hates the light, will not come into the light, for fear that his doings will be found out'* (John 3:17-20). To understand

this text, substitute truth for light. These first three I think you will agree are straightforward. The other three need a bit more explanation so we shall treat them separately.

23. OBSTINACY IN SIN

Obstinacy in sin owes its origin to two deadly sins: sensuality or lust, and sloth or even a combination of both. In the Book of Genesis, quite early on we have the story of the twin brothers Esau and Jacob. Esau is the embodiment of a man who is controlled by his sensuality. Coming in from a hard day's hunting in the fields he finds his brother stirring a delectable cooking-pot of broth. 'Give me some of your broth' he tells his brother Jacob. 'Only if you give me your birthright in return', replies Jacob. 'What use would my birthright be to me if I starve to death' is Esau's reply. It is not really logical: Esau has just weighed his birthright; that is to say, his God-given vocation against a mess of potage, and found that he preferred the satisfaction of his sensual appetite to God's Will for him. Later on, when Jacob plays another trick and deprives Esau of his father's blessing, Esau realizes what he has done and cries out and weeps. But Sacred Scripture says '*he could not be consoled*'. (*Gen 37:35*) Through his sensuality he sinned against the Holy Spirit. The moral of the story for us poor mortals is that we have to be on our guard against living a life dominated by sensuality where we pander to our physical appetites to such an extent that we lose our taste for the spiritual food of the love of God. If we give in like this, we can reach a point in which we cannot let go of the sensual attractions, which ultimately are converted into sins which are an abomination in God's sight. God cannot abide sin: He hates sin. As St. John Henry Newman said in one of his sermons to Mixed Congregations: '*He and It cannot be together and so He casts It into outer darkness*'. Now if the soul is inextricably bound to some sinful habit and is unable or unwilling to detach himself from it, he gets thrown out into the outer darkness. The concept comes across in the Parable of the Banquet where the man without the wedding garment is bound hand and foot and cast into the outer darkness. So, we see that it is not that God wants to condemn the soul to suffer in Hell but rather He throws the baby out with the bathwater, so-to-speak! If you won't let go of your sin, you will suffer the same fate. Above, I hinted at two reasons why we cling on to our sinful habits: we are unable or unwilling. The first mentioned is because of the deadly sin of lust. The second is <u>sloth.</u>

Sloth is one of the seven deadly sins. It is also called insensitivity of heart by St John Climacus as it was the main fault of the Israelites in the desert who kept on rejecting or neglecting the many graces God granted them. In us we may also call it lukewarmness, and like lukewarmness, it has two main characteristics: one, which we might call the obvious one, is negligence, or carelessness about little details, finishing things off and generally putting things off until a better time or opportunity occurs. The slothful man keeps on making resolutions which he never keeps. He will say to himself, 'I must eat less' and then in the very next meal eats twice as much. The second characteristic is attachment to venial sin. It is where a person has come to terms with his besetting fault and says to himself, 'this is the way I am so everybody, including God will have to put up with it'. Needless to say, there is no intention whatever of repenting and changing. He will say to himself, 'well I am still in a state of grace, so that's all right'. To begin with, what we have to bear in mind is that although venial sins do not kill off our life of grace, they paralyse it. We still have our supernatural life but it is apostolically useless. You see we need both grace and love.

At this point I think it is useful to bring forward a commentary on Matthew 25, 1-10. where we learn that grace is not charity but an effect of it. Matthew 25 presents to us the parable of the five wise and the five foolish virgins. As we all remember, when the Bridegroom is announced the foolish ones ask the wise ones to give them some oil. Now if the wise ones had been filled with the oil of charity, they would not have refused the foolish ones, but instead they said: '*go to those who sell*' (*Mt* 25:9). This shows that the oil is grace not charity. And the instruction 'go, rather, to those that sell' means 'go to the Church and her priests who, with the holy Sacraments, supply grace'. In case anyone should think I am making this up we have no less an authority than St Gertrude. In Chapter 55 of her Revelations we read: 'St Gertrude was deeply moved at the words '*Ecce sponsus venit*' and said to Our Lord: 'O most desirable Spouse! As I hear these words so frequently repeated, tell me how Thou wilt come, and what Thou wilt bring us?' He replied: 'I will now work with you and in you. Where is your lamp?' She replied: 'Behold, Lord, I will give Thee my heart for a lamp' He answered: 'I will fill it abundantly with oil -that is, with grace from My Heart'. She replied: 'But where is the wick to light it?' Our Lord replied: 'Your pure intention of doing everything for Me alone will be a wick, the light of which will be most pleasing to Me' (*Life and Revelations of St Gertrude*)

24. FINAL IMPENITENCE

If you study the Catholic Catechism carefully you will see that it lumps all the sins against the Holy Spirit together. Now, if there were a strong case for this it would seem to be placing Despair and Presumption as two aspects of Final Impenitence. However, I think not; for whilst the despairing person clings on to the idea that his sins are unforgiveable and the presumptuous person clings on to the idea that he does not need forgiveness, the person who is impenitent is attached to the sin itself and will not seek forgiveness. This person then is guilty of extreme <u>folly</u>; a folly that is produced by pride; he will not follow the example of the prodigal son and say to his Father: '*I have sinned against Heaven and before thee, I am not worthy to be called thy son!*' *(Luke 15:21)*. Just as there is rejoicing among the Angels over one sinner who repents; I am quite sure there must be the equivalent feeling of grief among the Angels over a sinner who refuses forgiveness (cf. Luke 15, 10). From this we can conclude that if a person is condemned to spend eternity suffering in Hell, then it is because of sheer foolishness. So, when the Psalm says: '*The fool has said in his heart, there is no God*' *(Ps 14:1)*, we have here the reason for his folly. This is because God alone can forgive. What we have to realize is that sins and sinfulness is all our own doing. The disasters and tribulations of the world are all our own doing. People are forever putting the blame on God for all the disasters and then will not turn to Him for forgiveness and remedy of their own folly. All this brings me to the **insight** corresponding to final impenitence and the eternity of suffering of Hell. St Thomas Aquinas who astutely observes: *'The eternity of pain does not correspond to the gravity of the guilt but it corresponds to the irreparable nature of the guilt'* (Summa I-II Q 87, art 5). How often have we heard people argue: how can God be just if He punishes someone forever in Hell for one mortal sin. But as we deduce from the above insight that you go to Hell not because of the sin but because of the state of soul you are in, which was produced by the sin. So, in effect, you are punished because you would not say sorry!

Consequently, I believe that if you were able to go into Hell and observe its inhabitants, you would find one soul in one corner saying: 'I was right; they were wrong' and another, 'I couldn't help it, 'people don't seem to realize and understand I had to kill him, there was no way out'.

25. SPIRITUAL ENVY

Of all the sins against the Holy Spirit this is the hardest to understand in my opinion. In the Parable of the labourers in the vineyard, where they all got paid one *denarius*, the reaction of the early labourers is quite understandable. But the Owner of the vineyard rebuked them saying: *'Why do you hate me because I am good'* (Mt 20:15). This, I think, is at the bottom of spiritual envy and why it is a sin against the Holy Spirit. It is a kind of hatred of goodness which is tantamount to hating God, the very worst of all sins (odium Deum).

Having been made out of nothing, we must realize that we have no rights, *vis-à-vis* God. So, it is in a mistaken attitude of pride where we are continually claiming our rights, that all our problems begin. Now in Heaven, among all the Saints, they are all delighted at the graces and glory of all their companions; they are happy because the others are happy. On earth we call it **charity** - the virtue that enables us to be pleased when others are more fortunate than we, whether materially or spiritually. It enables us to sympathise with others also in their misfortunes. Well the opposite reaction of sadness on seeing others' good fortune or feeling of joy on seeing others fall, is quite simply diabolical. As it says in the Book of Wisdom 2, 25: *'It was the Devil's envy* *which brought sin into the world.'* You remember one of Aesop's Fables: a young fox lost his tail in a trap and he then approached all the other foxes suggesting they should cut theirs off too, arguing that it enabled you to run faster and not be seen etc. But then a wily, old fox said, you are only saying that because you have lost your tail and don't want to seem a fool. When the Devil fell, he must have realized straightaway that he had made the most foolish error imaginable, but too late. In his anger and envy, he uses every available opportunity to lead us into sin. There is the origin of spiritual envy.

26. TRANSCENDING THE ABYSS

In order to cross over from earth to Heaven we have, so-to-speak, to cling on to Christ's coat-tails. As I think I mentioned before, we are not redeemed by the Cross alone, but by Christ's glorious Resurrection and Ascension into Heaven. *'I go to prepare a place for you'* (Jn 14:3) He said. But how do you hold on to Christ and get carried away up into Heaven? Through charity of course. In his first Epistle to the Corinthians in Chapter 13, St Paul praises this virtue. *'At the end we shall have done with faith and hope, but charity will remain'.* The reason is that it applies, or, if you like, functions in both the predicamental and transcendental orders and so is able to cross the abyss. If we live by love; if we practise charity, then we shall pass smoothly from this life into that Life; the Life of God in Heaven.

The basic temptation man has to face in life is the desire to be his own boss; that is why he runs away from God. This was the Devil's temptation. As we know from St Thomas Aquinas, Lucifer was the highest in the order of the Cherubim, that is, the most intelligent of angels and therefore the most intelligent of all God's creatures. Why then, you ask, this talk of folly? Surely that would be last thing Lucifer would be capable of? He did not, of course, say to himself 'I am equal to God' but he could say 'I am grown up now, I can manage by myself' and make a unilateral declaration of independence. As a matter of fact, the way things are, no creature is able to <u>implement</u> such a declaration; even an angel cannot cut himself off from God because he wills it.

Unfortunately, he managed to get Adam to try to do that and as we know left us his offspring in, so-to-speak, no-man's land. So, we find ourselves shot through with this overweening desire to operate independently of God. We are full of self-love; we always want our own way. This blinds our reason. How can God know what is good for us? So, then, once we have decided we know best and have all that we need to satisfy our yearnings for happiness, we start to look around and find others are better off than we are. So then from the deadly sin of pride, we are filled with envy like Cain in the Bible.

He then became angry with his brother and so smitten with another deadly sin: anger. And so it goes on and of course it is not confined to one or two individuals. We have entire nations full of greed and envy of their neighbours and make war on them. It is not my intention to study the social aspect of sin, but I am sure it is quite clear to everybody who thinks a little why we get ourselves globally into such a mess. Sin begets sin and brings disaster in its train. What is the answer? The answer has already been given: by Our Lord Jesus Christ. He is the Light of the world. This Light is the truth about God and ourselves; that we have no other solution but to turn back to God. Like the Prodigal Son we made our unilateral declaration of independence, and now, wallowing in the mud of the pig-sty we have made of our own lives, and the beautiful world God has created, we must return to our Father's house.

Christ said: *'I am the Way, the Truth and the Life. Anyone who follows Me will remain in darkness no longer'* (*Jn 14: 1-3*). The darkness is our self-centredness; always consulting our own pleasure and preference in order to reach happiness. When we share in Christ's Life and Love, then we consult our Father-God's pleasure and preference. *'I always do the will of my Father'* (*Jn 8:29*) said Our Lord, which consisted in giving His life for us to make us happy. But we cannot sit back and just sunbathe in God's Light and Love; we have to imitate Christ's Life of Love. We must forsake this love of self that is so demeaning and embrace the Love of God, and love like Him. *'Love one another as I have loved you'* (*Jn 13:34*). Jesus said, which, of course, means sacrificing ourselves for others as Jesus did.

27. SHARING

George Bernard Shaw was a cynical so-and-so. In his play *Man and Superman,* he has one of his characters say he would rather be in Hell than in Heaven. Why? Because the people there would be more interesting and so it would not be as boring as Heaven. Aside from the fact that the most interesting people who have ever lived on earth are the Saints, the inhabitants of Hell are all, one might say, by definition, the most selfish of God's creatures and therefore would not dream of sharing their supposed personal attractions and talents but would keep them all to themselves. The Saints, on the other hand, are practised in the art of self-giving and so whatever gifts they have they are willing to share with others. This little **insight** occurs in many places in the Gospel and Our Lord slots it into His parables and stories. In the one about a woman losing the coin in her house and sweeping it until she finds it, she is reported as saying: *'Rejoice with me because I have found the coin I had lost' (Lk 15:9).* So, you see we have to share everything we have that is good, including our joys. Follow the example of Our Lady who visits her cousin Elizabeth after the Annunciation. Of course, we must not spread the bad things: diseases, doctrinal errors and sin.

28. INTERIOR LIFE: FATHER LACORDAIRE

Our Lord has taught us how to live and so we have to meditate on His words and His actions. But it is not enough just to look at Him from the outside, so-to-speak. We have to try to get inside and see what goes on in that exquisite mind and that loving heart. We have, if you will pardon the expression, to get under His skin. Father Lacordaire the famous French Dominican Preacher of the 19th Century in his *'Life of Jesus Christ'* says:

> *'There are two lives –the outer life and the inner life. The outer life would be nothing without the inner life. The inner life is the support of the other and therefore desiring*

> to study the life of Jesus Christ I must begin by examining his inner life.
>
> But what is this inner life? It is the converse between ourselves and ourselves. Every man converses with himself. Every man, every intelligent being holds this inner converse with himself, which forms his real life. The inner life is - in a sense - the whole man, and forms the worth of man'.

What a wonderful **insight** which has been used by several authors since his time. It is not surprising to find the same idea in '*Our Saviour and His Love for us*' by Garrigou-Lagrange.

The great significance of this **insight** is that it tells us about Our Lord's real life, namely a loving conversation with the other two Persons of the Blessed Trinity: the Father and the Holy Spirit. If we read the Holy Gospel carefully, we will find Our Lord continually referring to His heavenly Father. '*Father I say this not for myself, but for those standing around*'; '*Father I know you hear me at all times*'; '*Father, save me from undergoing this hour of trial*'; '*Father, forgive them for they know not what they do*'.

But it has yet another very significant consequence for us too, for it shows us how we must have an <u>interior life</u>. To begin with, let us be clear that this inner conversation goes on all the time inside every intelligent being as Father Lacordaire says. Apart from our own experience of how from the moment we get up in the morning we start talking to ourselves, we have it in the Holy Gospel. Do you remember the Parable of the Unjust Steward, how, when he was sacked by his master said within himself, '*to beg I am ashamed*' (Lk 16:3). Now, obviously, the quality of this inner conversation varies enormously from person to person. Some people have a very low-level dialogue with sensual objects; others contemplate reprisals and revenge on those they regard as their enemies; others criticize others interiorly and look down on others' conversation, appearance, dress manners etc. etc. Now clearly, the good Christian should have an uplifting, even edifying inner conversation in such a way that, if they were to express their inner conversation externally so others would hear them, those other persons would be edified and not scandalized. But what about the saintly Christian? Well, he should reflect the inner peace of his soul and the inner conversation with God. I said at the start of this little essay how in theology if one did not understand the meaning of <u>grace</u>, one would not get very far in theology. Well, now I have to say that without living the life of grace one would not get very far along the road to sanctity. Question: has a newly baptized baby a life of grace? Answer: of course. But has this newly baptized baby interior life? Answer: No! This comes when we get to the use of reason and we reflect on the reality of the life of grace, and recognize the fact that the Blessed Trinity is living within us and we converse with each one of the Three Divine Persons: the Father, the Son and the Holy Spirit. So, we can conclude that this should be our aim in life, to hold a loving conversation within with God and be contemplative souls.

29. THE HOLY SPIRIT

The Holy Spirit has an awful lot to do with the progress and development of this interior life of the Christian soul. Furthermore, we realize that one day this inner conversation, which corresponds to something kept hidden from others, will come out into the open when we reach Heaven. There, all the inhabitants of Heaven converse freely and openly with God and enter into the loving Inner Conversation of the Three Divine Persons: the Divine Dialogue.

Well now, this loving familiarity between the three Divine Persons is based on Love, which we might call the Holy Spirit's role par excellence. Father Farrell suggests another **insight**, (which, I suspect, he has taken from St Thomas Aquinas). He tells us that the Holy Spirit's rôle, regarding our interior life, is to give us the warmth and sense of familiarity with the things of God. He writes *'God has given man the supernatural infused virtues to enable man to produce those divine-human acts which lead to the vision of God. But His generosity to man has not stopped here. The world of the supernatural is familiar to God. It is His own world. But it is not familiar to man. If man is to make his way safely and easily in the world of the supernatural, he must be led by God. Human reason is a sufficient guide to man in the natural world of man.*

But in the world of God human reason, even when it is perfected by faith, is not an accurate guide. Human reason can enable man to live familiarly with other men and with his inferiors, the animals, the plants and the earth itself. But God is infinite perfection. Human reason alone cannot give man that familiarity with God which will enable him to act easily and safely in the world of the supernatural. To overcome this difficulty, to make man's progress in God's world easy, God has given man the gifts, fruits and beatitudes of the Holy Spirit.' (Fr Walter Farrell, *'My Way of Life'*).

30. THE INSIGHT OF POWER

Strictly speaking, I have no quotation to back up what I have to say now. Whenever I preach to priests about their special vocation to the priesthood, the thought that springs to mind is <u>power</u>. Perhaps this is because when you think of a Bishop, who has the plenitude of the Priesthood, you also have the plenitude of priestly power. Anyway, as we all know, in the ecclesiastical world, they are the ones who have the power: the Bishops. Consequently, if one is looking for a suitable candidate for the Bishopric, you must look for someone who knows how to exercise power. Some lack fortitude and do not use the power as they ought. Others are proud and are too authoritarian. They obviously need prudence and discretion to know when to speak and when to keep quiet. It is a difficult job.

Well, my concern is not to be giving Bishops advice about how to do their job, but to draw a conclusion not just for priests who also are endowed with an awe-inspiring amount of power and which they have to administer with prudence and discretion, but for lay-people who are Christians. This is because the Christian faithful have a priestly soul: just consider the first point of *The Forge* by St Josemaría Escriva:

> 'We are children of God, bearers of the only flame that can light up the paths of the earth for souls, of the only brightness which can never be darkened, dimmed, or overshadowed.
>
> The Lord uses us as torches, to make that light shine out. Much depends on us; if we respond many people will

> *remain in darkness no longer, but will walk instead along paths that lead to eternal life.'*

When we get to Heaven we shall share in God's own Life; but this means God's own Power. As I said earlier on, in God everything is one. Consequently, if you had some individual let loose in Heaven with all that Power and no sense of responsibility, we would have Hell instead of Heaven. This is why the formula for real Canonisation – as often suggested by St Josemaría - is *'Well done, good and faithful servant, because you have been faithful over little things, enter into the joy of your Lord'* (Mt 25:23).

Life on earth is not a test or trial organized by God to see what stuff we are made of, given the fact that He made us and so knows us perfectly well, but for us to learn to love as He has loved, to serve others and exercise the great powers that have been entrusted to us with our priestly soul. So, we have to pray and sacrifice ourselves for others and teach them the ways of God and the ways to God and prove ourselves worthy of Him.

PART II

Now we start a new section which contains further **insights** which are akin to the riches to be found in Jesus Christ referred to by St Paul when writing to the Ephesians. St John of the Cross speaks of them and explains how they can be reached only through the Cross. St Josemaría would probably say by entering the wounds of Jesus on the Cross, in particular, the Fifth Wound made by the Centurion's spear. Through this wound we reach the Sacred Heart of Jesus which contains all the riches of his Love,

FIRST STEP: CREATION AND FALL

THERE ARE TWO ASPECTS TO creation. The creation of man, and the creation of the world. The Book of Genesis in Chapter 2 says *'Let us make man to our image and likeness' (Gen 1:26)*. This means that Adam and Eve were, as far as their human nature was concerned, similar to God. We all remember how the penny catechism tells us that this likeness is chiefly in our soul. Well, in my opinion, this refers to the <u>image</u> of God and as the Catechism says, just as there are three Persons in one God, there are three powers of the soul, namely, the intellect, the will and the memory. This, I believe comes from St Augustine. Some purist might well say: but there are only two spiritual powers - the intellect and the will; the memory belongs to the sensitive powers and so is material. At this point, I think it is appropriate to include St Augustine's words on Creation from his book, the City of God, Book XI, Chapter 25:

> *'I know that in practice, we ought to say that a person <u>enjoys</u> what he produces but merely <u>makes use</u> of. The point of this distinction seems to be that a thing enjoyed is related directly to ourselves and not to something else, whereas a thing used is sought as a means to some other end. Thus, we may say that he who can doubt that, when things are loved, the loving of them is also true and certain? Further, just as there is no-one who does not wish to be happy, so there is no-one who does not wish to exist. For, how can anyone be happy if he does not exist?*

> *Merely to exist is, by the very nature of things, so pleasant in itself it is enough to make even the wretched unwilling to die; for even when they are conscious of their misery, what they want to put an end to is not themselves but the misery. This is even the case with those who merely feel miserable but manifestly are so, men who seem fools in the eyes of the wise, and paupers and beggars to those who consider themselves well off. For, if they had a choice between personal immortality, in which their unhappiness would never end, or complete and permanent annihilation if they objected to eternal misery, they would be delighted to choose to live forever in misery rather than not to exist at all.*
>
> *If proof were needed, appeal can be made to the well-known feeling of these men. They are afraid to die, and prefer to live on in misfortune rather than to end it by death. This is proof enough that nature shrinks from annihilation. If proof be needed how much human nature loves to know and hates to be mistaken, recall that there is not a man who would not rather be sad but sane, than glad but mad. Now, this great and marvellous light of love and hate is peculiar to man alone among all living animals.'*

So much for St Augustine. It could be the reader finds his words hard to follow, but in any event, one has to concede that nobody else has ever given such a convincing argument in favour, if that is the right word, of hell. Although this subject will crop up again, when we come to consider the Last Things, Hell is such a difficult mystery to come to terms with, that it has to be admitted that St Augustine's thoughts are deep.

However, now we have finished the digression which was St Augustine's mind on the similarity of man's soul to the being of God, we can now add a few words from St Thomas Aquinas, not so much about the similarity between man and God as the confirmation that he does accept the idea of an intellective memory for, as it happens, St Thomas does put forward the idea that the intellect, which is spiritual, performs the function of retaining things, which can be called spiritual memory. So now we can say that God raised these powers to be like himself, making them supernatural. This is the preternatural gift of grace, which at the end of life is transformed into the <u>likeness</u> of God referred to in Genesis. So, during our lifetime we would, like Adam and Eve, be called by God to develop this life of grace and at the end see it transformed into the <u>lumen gloriae</u>, the light of glory when the soul will be able to contemplate God. This would appear to be the meaning of St John's. *'Beloved, we are sons of God, even now, and what we shall be hereafter, has not been made known as yet. But we know that when he comes we shall be like him; we shall see him, as he is' (1 Jn 3:2).* This way, we may dare to say that by stating we are made to God's image, is a statement of fact, and that to say made to his likeness, is a statement of intent. Creation of the world: God did not just create man, but the world to live in, and all the other things that exist. And how beautiful it all is, how wonderful God must be if he made all these beautiful things. It is said that Our Lady at the age of three, (bearing in mind that since she was exempt from original sin, must have been exceptionally intelligent and so realised that all the beautiful things in the world, all the blessings bestowed on the chosen people, and all the graces she herself had received from God), burst forth in a song of praise to God, to thank and bless him for all his gifts, and as a consequence resolved to spend her life praising and loving him. Not hard to believe. This consideration has led me to conclude that the worst thing about modern day scientists who put forward their theories about the origin of the world, sin by rejecting the notion that God has made the world out of nothing, thereby depriving God of the credit of creating the world. Now it stands to reason that if you say God did not create the world but it somehow created itself, you are not giving God his glory. But, as we know from the Sacred Scripture, God created the world and all that is in it, for his glory. All we have to do is follow the words of Jesus in the Gospel: *'Consider the lilies of the field. Solomon in all his glory was not arrayed like one of these' (Mt 6:29).* Here, may I be allowed an aside. We know that Leibniz, who was a very accomplished mathematician and invented calculus, was still ignorant enough to say, since God was perfect, the world we live in is the most perfect it is possible to make. I have not been to America, and being very English, I would be tempted to claim that the garden of England, has the most beautiful flowers in the world. How foolish that would be, as there is no doubt that in America they have got all our flowers and many more besides. So why should God not be able to create many more?

Of course, you might retort, this is where the modern scientists catch you out. Have you not heard they have invented lots of parallel universes? And if that were a typically absurd suggestion, what about finding another planet with oxygen and an atmosphere like ours capable of sustaining life? This is where reasoning has to call a halt to these flights of fancy, the exquisite balance of everything in the world, demands that the probability of finding such a planet is one in a million. The clinching argument, however, comes from theology, for as we know, there is only one Jesus Christ, and we have got him, it is impossible that there should be a parallel universe in which God becomes incarnate a second time.

But why did God create the world, and all the other things in it? God created the world for his glory and his glory is realised on creating man. The things in the world are like a ladder upon which a man climbs to reach the heights of Heaven and to be with God. *'Increase and multiply and fill the earth' (Gen 1:28)* he said to Adam. That is to say, make use of all the things of the earth and thereby give me glory. First, recognise and acknowledge that I have created all these for you, to show you my love and to enable you to understand my love for you. The creation of the world is like the gift a lover makes to his beloved. This the first element in God's design or plan of our salvation, and the second is that depending on how we treat these created things, we make a reciprocal offering to our Father God. In his Spiritual Exercises, St Ignatius of Loyola, expresses it succinctly:

> *'Man was created to praise, do reverence to and serve God, and thereby save his soul. And the other things on the face of the earth were created for man's sake and to help him on to his end for which he was created. Hence it follows that man should make use of creatures so far as they do help him towards his end, and should withdraw from them in so far as they are a hindrance to him in regard of that end'.*

THE DEVIL'S TEMPTATION OF EVE

WHAT HAS GONE BEFORE IS put into perspective by the description in the Book of Genesis of how Eve was tempted by the Devil and led into sin. He is the Father of lies, and that is how he tempted Eve. But he did not just tell a lie. He asked a question which enclosed a lie. *'What is this command God has given you not to eat the fruit of any tree in the garden?'* *(Gen 2:16)*. And, as St Francis de Sales says, Eve spoke and was lost.

When you are asked a pseudo-question you must remain silent, otherwise you consent to the untruth enclosed within the question. Eve is being very polite in answering the question. But she should have just trampled on the serpent instead. By answering, she was giving tacit agreement to what the Devil had implied, namely, that God was somehow unfair, fancy not allowing them to eat the fruit of any tree in the garden, why that is outrageous! He cannot be good if he makes such demands. We know, Eve knew, in fact everybody knows, that God is good and does not make outrageous demands but the suggestion has been made, the line has been cast and the fish has bitten and swallowed the bait and is caught.

This is not surprising, coming from the Devil. He was, if we are to believe St Thomas the highest in the Order of the Cherubim who stand for the cleverest of all God's Angels. So, this is the equivalent of saying the most highly endowed of God's creatures. So, I say, is it not surprising that Satan, or Lucifer, should say to himself, 'I know I am not as bright and beautiful as you, God, but I am at least clever enough to know my own mind and love myself enough to know what is good for me. I can manage perfectly well by myself thank you very much. I love myself sufficiently to ensure my own happiness'. But this is where he went wrong. In the course of his own declaration of unilateral sufficiency he was indirectly discounting God and furthermore discounting God's love. God's love is infinite and all-embracing. He loves all of us more than we love ourselves. This is the basic essential act of faith required of all God's creatures, not just us poor human creatures but angels as well, who, we have to acknowledge, are far more intelligent than we are. Now, this is so important I think I should repeat it. God loves me, more than I love me. As a consequence, he knows best what is best for me. In fact, he has created the world, all human creatures and angels, for the simple purpose of making them happy. We may think that following our own way, doing our own thing, is the path to happiness. It is, however, a grave error. And if we persistent in it, mortal sin. So, this is what Eve did, and having tasted the apple, or whatever the fruit was, gave some to her husband and he ate with her. Just as an aside, if Adam had rejected Eve's gesture, and maintained his integrity, everything would have been fine, unfortunately as the head of the human race he landed us all in the mire. Why did he succumb? There can only be one answer to that and that is his love for Eve. He sinned because she had sinned.

Trying to go a bit deeper into the psychology of this disaster, it seems to me that Adam and Eve failed to appreciate what God had done for them until that moment. He had created them, filled them with all sorts of qualities and on top of that given them the supernatural gift of grace. Everything short of letting them see his face.

This means the preternatural gift of grace was not definitive, which means it could be lost and as we have seen was in fact lost. Something similar applies to Lucifer for, according to some author, I once read, if Lucifer had seen God's face, he would not have rejected him. It could well be of course that this author whose name I forget was inferring this from the knowledge that when once in Heaven we contemplate the face of God, we cannot not love him, and so this would apply to all the angels as well.

CONSEQUENCES OF THE FALL

WHEN ONCE ADAM AND EVE had fallen into sin, the immediate effect was loss of sanctifying grace. Nowadays, some translations of the Sacred Scripture insist on using the word favour instead of the time-honoured theological term, <u>grace</u>. But here it has its usefulness, because we can say, Adam fell out of favour with God. The beneficial influence of the union between man and God was lost, so that man's faculties went out of sync. We find that man is now able to suffer and to die. His passions are out of control: he is subject to irascibility and concupiscence. And on top of this, because man is supposed to be in charge of the whole of creation, it too makes its protest. St Paul says *'The whole of creation groans in common travail all the while'* (Rom 8:22).

When he goes to till the earth, it yields him thorns and thistles. It too has lost the beneficial influence of God. Once more I subject you to a digression, for it is here that Martin Luther went astray, for he made original sin and its consequences the same. He confused them to such an extent that wherever he found the effects of original sin he said that original sin itself was there. What conclusion did he draw from this error? Well, that even though we are baptised, and therefore have no original sin any more, if you find you have the consequences like being scatter-brained, or in pain, or diseased, then you are in a state of sin. So how do you say you have been redeemed by Christ's sacrifice? Because he prevents you from feeling the heat of God's wrath. Christ has paid the ransom by shedding his blood, but instead of washing away your sins, he has simply covered them over. In fact, Luther used the comparison taken from the Book of Leviticus in the Old Testament of the scapegoat. This means that just as in the days of the trek through the desert, if in any camp someone sinned, then they would take a goat, shave it and beat it scampering out of the camp carrying the sin and its guilt. So, this is what Christ has done for us; simply taken our guilt on his own shoulders; we remain sinful, however. It is as if Christ were like an umbrella, the wrath of Almighty God rains down on the human race, but we don't get wet because Christ intervenes and keeps us from getting wet. What is the consequence of this reasoning? To begin with, we are still sinful and have not received sanctifying grace, as we are taught in the Catholic Church; we just escape the punishment we deserve for our sins. (P.S. perhaps this is the reason why Michael Schmaus once said that if you did not understand the concept of grace you would not be able to understand Catholicism). A more subtle consequence is that once Christ has died on the Cross, we are saved. Whether he rises from the dead or not does not matter anymore, whereas the good Catholic will say, I need Christ to rise from the dead to put me in a state of grace. We can also deduce from this, why Anglican theologians are not put out by someone who has claimed to find the remains of Christ, which would of course mean that he had not risen from the dead. Really, because the resurrection is irrelevant. How they can say this in the face of St Paul's Epistle to the Corinthians which says if Christ is not risen, we remain in our sins, I do not know. Do we not say in one of the prefaces and what is said in one of the Acclamations after the Consecration in Mass: *'Dying you destroyed our death, rising you restored our life'*. Of course, this train of thought was pursued by John Calvin who went on to say, that if you were with him in Geneva, you would be saved; you were, so-to-speak, under Calvin's umbrella, keeping out of the rain -of the wrath of God -, but if not you would be damned. This is the teaching of Predestinationism, and it was spread about in Scotland by John Knox. How can this teaching be reconciled with belief in a good and compassionate God? If you are predestined for Heaven, all is fine, you cannot go wrong. You are essentially good, whereas if you are predestined for Hell, you cannot do right, you are born bad and remain so. Nowadays, not just Evangelicals and Presbyterians subscribe to this absurd doctrine, but practically everybody. Just witness the Hollywood pictures. I am afraid I am not up to date with the latest ones, but when I was young it was abundantly clear that the Indians were bad and the cowboys good. Why? Because God has actually made them so. So, where does free will come in? Somewhere along the line it has been disposed of. At this point we need to stop and think of why God has taken away the original sin but left us with the consequences.

EFFECT OF THE CONSEQUENCES OF ORIGINAL SIN

WE NOW ASK 'BUT WHY' did not God take away the consequences of original sin as well as the sin itself'? In the 'Our Father', which is the prayer which Jesus himself composed, the sixth petition is 'lead us not into temptation'. Of course, it isn't God himself who leads us into temptation. The Scripture makes this abundantly clear. Our enemies are the world, the flesh and the Devil. God allows these enemies to attack us and lead us into sin. I am sure that in the introduction to the Book of Job, which we find in the Old Testament, when God speaks proudly of his son, holy Job, he does the same with each one of us; that is, he speaks highly of each one of his sons, and challenges the Devil to test his integrity and fidelity to his Father God. I think that it is as it were in the New Dispensation, each of his sons who will ultimately qualify for entry into Heaven, has to prove himself. This is not done for the sake of bravado, of course but, as always, to manifest the glory of God. Each one of us, remember, has to show himself, as a true son of God, and, as it says in point 265 in *The Way*, by St Josemaría, is called to '*uphold the royal dignity*'. And how is this done without a test? To my mind, this is reminiscent of the opening words of *The Way* which end saying '….. *and so become a soul of worth*' (I think that in later translations this is different, however this version suits my train of thought). God is a proud father and wants us to reflect his high standard of holiness. I remember some time ago, reading St Brigitte of Sweden's revelations about Our Lady who I think praises John the Baptist for his exceedingly great chastity, indicating that this gives great glory to God, as indeed did holy Job. I would think also that something similar must be true of the Holy Angels; they too must have passed through the test of being worthy of God. But no-one really knows what this would consist in, except to say, it would be in some respects similar to our testing in that it has to do with the measure of our love of God, and to have been achieved through complete reliance on God and his grace. This observation, namely, that if we are to come through the test with flying colours, is provoked by the awareness that there is one Saviour, and it is through his grace we are able to attain holiness, for without him we can do nothing. These things, making these observations, helps us to draw the conclusions for our ascetical struggle, in particular that it will not be an easy passage, that it is the same for everybody. That means, we all are endowed with free will, and all have to rely on God's grace, which we receive thanks to Our Lord and Saviour, Jesus Christ Our Lord. Everything about our test is related to what Our Lord has done for us.

GOD'S PLAN OF REDEMPTION

ST AUGUSTINE, I THINK I am right in saying, declared that God had foreseen all that we have described: that man would succumb to the Devil's wiles, and fall into sin. And then, what's more, deserve to be cast into Hell, prepared for the Devil and his Angels. (In the Book of Revelation, it says that the devil's tail dragged down a third of the stars of Heaven, presumably meaning the fallen angels, now devils). This means that all of us, children as we are of Adam and Eve, would be therefore deprived of that life of grace we were destined to inherit from them. But, St Augustine argued, how could it be possible that a Just God, would create all of us human creatures, just to be cast into hell, to suffer endlessly? Therefore, He must have had a plan in mind. We, no doubt, could well have called it a contingency plan, or, as they say in the sporting world 'plan B'. This could not be the way God would work however, nor is it how it is expressed in the Documents of the Second Vatican Council in the Dogmatic Constitution of the Church *Lumen Gentium*, n.2, which I propose to quote again:

> *'The plan of the eternal Father's wisdom and goodness is utterly free; it is his secret: he created the whole world, decided to raise men to a share in the divine life. He did not abandon them when, in Adam, they fell, for he has continually offered them help to salvation having Christ, the Redeemer, in view, 'who is the image of the invisible God, the first-born of all creation' (Col 1:15). All those the Father chose before time began, 'those whom he foreknew*

> *he also predestined to be conformed to the image of his Son, in order that he might be the first-born among many brethren"* (Rom 8:29).

In other words, when we come into the world, then are baptised, our purpose should be to cultivate this supernatural life which has graciously been restored to us thanks to the generosity of Our Lord and Saviour, Jesus Christ. It just so happens, however, that unless we are especially precocious, we do not wake up to the fact of being God's children and endowed with His grace until we come to the use of reason.

That is why theologians who specialise in the spiritual life have coined a new expression. They distinguish between the <u>supernatural</u> life, which is there for as long as we remain free from mortal sin. (Mortal sin is so called because it is the kind of sin which causes the death of the soul. Mortal is from the Latin for death: *mors/mortis)*. When we have <u>interior</u> life, it is where the person, now fully aware of the importance and indeed the beauty of the supernatural life, deliberately cultivates the growth and development of the supernatural life; imitating Jesus Christ, acquiring His virtues, engaging in the struggle not to give in to the temptations of the world, the flesh and the devil, and so become a living saint and worthy of eternal happiness and union with Almighty God.

At the very beginning, before God had created mankind, we are saying he wanted men to be his children, made to his image and likeness. But as we know, endowed as they were with freedom, they chose, at the instigation of the devil, to disobey God and fall into sin. Because Adam and Eve were the parents of the whole human race all their offspring were then deprived of grace. The contingency plan which we have just discussed that the Second Person of the Blessed Trinity, the Word, became flesh and by doing so, on the one hand, provided us with an example in his own person for us to follow, and also made it possible for him to die and offer his life for us. The result is that we were able to receive the grace we had lost through the sin of our first parents, and then struggle during our life-time to live our lives as children of God. Now, whereas in the original design of God, we would collectively have been in a state of grace, and then been able to share in God's life as a natural sequence of our condition. In the contingency economy living a supernatural life is only accessible through personal and individual choice and struggle, and can only achieve fulfilment as a supernatural end, as members of the Mystical Body of Christ. The achievement, if we can call it that, of natural purpose is closed to us. In the final analysis, it results in only some being saved and others lost.

THE NARROW GATE

IN THE GOSPEL OF ST Matthew, it says *'Make your way in by the narrow gate. It is a broad gate and a wide road that leads to perdition, and those who go in that way are many indeed; but how small is the gate, how narrow the road that leads on to life, and how few there are that find it!' (Mt 7:13).*

These words give us a lot of food for thought. Of course, it leads to a great deal of speculation about how many will be saved; a number which I am sure Our Lord would say is known only by His Father. When we look around us today and see the sins being committed and very serious sins, so many abortions, so much overt sexuality, hedonism is rife, and abuse of children, which Our Lord said would be punished by tying a millstone round the neck of the perpetrators. The mind boggles; and yet on the other hand we know how loving and forgiving Our Lord is, and how many come back to Him with repentance. A few years ago, we celebrated the Jubilee Year of Divine Mercy and the Pope spoke a great deal about it. Pope St John Paul II wrote his second Encyclical about Mercy in *'Dives in Misericordia'*. This in turn was quite probably inspired by the communications of St Faustina Kowalska about this time of mercy in the life of the Church. Saint Josemaría was quite probably influenced by another holy nun, Madre Esperanza del Amor Misericordioso (Alhama Valero), foundress of the Slaves of Merciful Love, and promoter of the devotion to the Merciful Love of Jesus. Her Congregation was approved by the Sacred Congregation of Religious in 1949 and received the *Decretum Laudis* in 1970. She constructed the Shrine of Merciful Love in Collevalenza, which was visited by Pope St John Paul II in 1981. All of which leads us to take a more optimistic view of the outcome of those to be judged on departing this life.

But now, what do we reckon is this <u>narrow gate</u>? Briefly, I think it means the pains and sufferings of this present life. St John of the Cross says quite simply that it is the Cross of Our Lord. I feel sure he is not using the words of the precious Gospel just that we can amuse ourselves speculating about how many will go to heaven and how many will go to hell. It is, in effect, a complete waste of time for us to bother our heads about that. He is teaching us, as usual, about a very practical thing which is our <u>attitude</u> once more in approaching our spiritual life. In this case, our approach to the trials, difficulties and sufferings of life because, so frequently, we shy away from them and choose the easy way out. No matter who we are, rich or poor, no matter what age we are, young or old, we all have to suffer. In the Book of Genesis, after the Fall, the dire predictions of God, as a consequence of sin, are directed to the human race universally, without any exceptions whatsoever. God subjects each one of us to trials or tests of our faith and trust in Him. Are we going to be like our first parents, or are we going to be like our Saviour Jesus Christ, and His loving Mother Mary who is our Mother too? Adam and Eve failed and disobeyed God, Jesus and Mary overcame all the difficulties and came through triumphant.

We have to acknowledge that there is a difference between Jesus and us. He is God after all, but it is also true that He fought the good fight in His human nature. And, if we want take an example of someone who has only a human nature and is not God, we have Our Lady. Then, again, we have a whole army of Saints in Heaven who are a wonderful example for us and who were exactly the same as we are in every respect and quite a number of them followed a path which was leading to perdition until they came to their senses and repented of their foolish and evil ways. In this, as always, we have to choose which way we are going to travel the path of life. When Our Lord says 'make your way in the narrow gate', he is in effect saying: 'embrace the Cross'. It is what He said on another occasion: 'if anyone would come after me, let him deny himself and take up his cross daily and follow me' *(Lk 9:23)*. But will we?

One of our problems is self-pity. The cross comes in the shape of a great pile of work which tires us out. Or it could be we receive some very sad news which makes us depressed. Somebody we were relying on to help us in our work and other difficulties leaves us abandoned. And what do we say? We say I have suffered enough and switch on the television, or pick up the newspaper, and avoid the cross.

In my opinion, this has a great deal to do with surprise. It seems to us that the extra amount of work which we weren't expecting is like the last straw which broke the camel's back, it is too much. Now this, in turn, is because of our failure to be prepared.

Our Lord gives us all these sayings and recommendations in the Holy Gospel and on top of that presents us with Himself, a portrait in pain, on the Cross, in the hope that the message will penetrate - we have to embrace His Holy Cross, so that when the time comes we will accept it generously. In other words, we have to cultivate in our hearts a love of the Holy Cross of Jesus. St Josemaría was well aware of this and encouraged us to meditate on the Cross. There is that interesting point in *The Way* which speaks about the cross without its crucified:

> *'When you see a poor wooden Cross, alone, uncared for and of no value... and without its Crucified, don't forget that that Cross is your Cross: the Cross of each day, the hidden Cross, without splendour or consolation..., which is awaiting the Crucified it lacks: and that Crucified must be you'. (The Way, no. 178)*

St Josemaría, as we know, had a Cross without a figure on it, placed at the entrance of the oratories of the centres of Opus Dei to remind people of this. In addition, as we know, also in the early days of his ministry with young people he came in contact with, he would insist that they carry a crucifix around with them. When he attended his first circle (a 'circle' is a class of spiritual and doctrinal formation which Opus Dei offers to people) in Barcelona in 1939, Rafael Termes tells of how St Josemaría asked him if he had a crucifix and when he said he hadn't, St Josemaría said to Isidoro, one of the first members of Opus Dei (I think it was Isidoro Zorzano who accompanied him on that occasion) **'*you give your crucifix to Rafael, we can get another one for you when we get back to Madrid*'**. This tells how much it meant to St Josemaría that we all have a crucifix with us all the time. In this way also we are able to kiss it when things get hard. And what is the idea of all this? Well, to be prepared of course, for when we reject the Cross, that is, fail to enter through the narrow gate. That's because the difficulties, the bereavement, the financial loss, the extra burden of work, came upon us all of a sudden. We were taken by surprise and reacted *primo primi* with an instinctive, animal-like reaction, and threw it away. The opportunity was lost. One of the things I learnt in hospital was that just as the joys and the perks of life come and go very quickly, so do the pains and sorrows. And what happens is that we miss out on golden opportunities to offer sacrifices to God. No sooner does the pain begin, then it disappears. I am not saying that things like arthritis, sciatica or lumbago, disappear quickly, but most set-backs, sorrows and disappointments do. This means that in our nightly moment of examination of conscience it is sometimes a good idea to look back over the day and ask ourselves about the difficulties and pains of the day to find out if we offered them up. They are like caresses from Our Lord. On the day Pope St John Paul II was shot, and he was in hospital, Blessed Alvaro went to visit him and said to the Pope, that he considered the incident had been like a caress from Our Lady, and the Pope said, 'that was just what I was thinking myself'!

When we mention St John Paul II, it brings to mind his total acceptance of the Cross in his final illness when he was afflicted with Parkinson's disease and accepted all the discomfort and pains that went with it. What was it that enabled him to accept it all? I am sure that it was voluntary mortification which he practised throughout his long life. A lot of people know, but for those who don't, it helps to remember one of his first trips abroad to the Philippines. It happened that in the convent he was to stay they needed extra staff to help the nuns to prepare things for the Holy Father and the entourage. Well, I have it on good authority that a number of women members of Opus Dei were brought in to help out and because they had not had time to clean the whole house, they thought they would leave the chapel to the end when everybody has gone to bed. But when they went back to the chapel at midnight, they found the Pope on the floor of the chapel with his arms outstretched, praying! And this was after a long and tiring flight across the world. Of course, I am not suggesting you or I take these extreme measures, but we can at least take note, make some examination of how ready we are for sacrifice and mortification in imitation of Our Lord and his Saints.

DIVINE FILIATION

A SECOND TOPIC FOLLOWING ON from the description of our fall into sin, is obviously divine filiation. We have seen that when once man had rejected God's original plan, he had no alternative but to conform to God's 'emergency plan' (although I don't like using that expression, especially after recording earlier St Augustine's explanation and quoting paragraph two of the Lumen Gentium which makes it explicit). This means falling in with God's plan to make us all his adoptive sons. In my second year in the Roman College of the Holy Cross, right at the beginning of a retreat, St Josemaría came and gave us a talk; I did not understand a great deal because my Spanish was not very good, but I do remember the opening phrase. He quoted the beginning of St Paul's Epistle to the Ephesians: *'He has chosen us out from the foundation of the world to be saints' (cf Eph 1:4)*. Blessed Columba Marmion in *'Christ, the Life of the Soul'*, has a very beautiful commentary on this and related passages which explain the theological basis of divine filiation:

> *Thus, not only has the Father chosen us from all eternity in His Christ: 'Elegit nos in ipso' - note the expression 'in ipso' - all that is apart from Christ does not exist, so to speak, in the Divine thought - but it is also by Jesus Christ that we receive grace, the means of the adoption He destines for us: 'Qui praedestinavit nos in adoptionem filiorum PER JESUM CHRISTUM' (Eph 4:15). We are sons, like Jesus, we by grace, He by nature; He, God's own Son, we His adopted sons: Et ipse filius et nos filii; ille proprius, nos adoptivi, sed ille salvat et nos salvamur.*

> *It is by Christ that we enter into God's family, it is from Him and by Him that grace and consequently Divine life come to us: Ego sum vita ...ego veni ut vitam habeant et abundantius habeant.*
>
> *Such is the very source of our holiness. As everything in Jesus Christ can be summed up in His Divine Sonship, thus everything in the Christian can be summed up in his participation of this sonship, by Jesus Christ, and in Jesus Christ... We must all be partakers of the holiness of Jesus. Christ excludes no one from the life He has brought and, by it, He renders us children of God.*

I feel sure that most people who read this will recall that it was in September 1931 that St Josemaría had a supernatural event which impressed the spirit of divine filiation deeply onto his soul. But it did not begin then. Some years ago, one of the members of Opus Dei who happened to be on a course in Molinoviejo (Spain) exclaimed in a get-together with St Josemaría, 'How pleasant it is to be here in the get-together' (it would have been 1947 or thereabouts) and the Father replied, **'yes, my son, but I did not see that on the 2ⁿᵈ October, like, for example the spirit of divine filiation'**. So, from this we can see that St Josemaría had the spirit of divine filiation from the start. It is not only an integral part of the spirit of Opus Dei, but its basis. As we know, the spirit of Opus Dei is to live unity of life, the spirit that leads us to convert all our activities into prayer and then by offering this prayer through the Holy Sacrifice of the Mass, into apostolate. Jesus was, is, perfect God and perfect Man. He is both. So, his human actions are at the same time divine, or we would say, supernatural. He cannot help but perform human actions which are in accordance with his heavenly Father's will, and be directed towards Heaven. We, on the other hand, are adoptive children of God, and much as we would like to make all our actions divine, they very often turn out to be just human, natural and not directed to God, or even pleasing to him. What is natural to Jesus, is supernatural to us and so we have to live out our divine filiation through which we convert the human into the divine. To do this, we need to keep on remembering God's presence and that, as it says in *The Way* no. 267

'*He is there like a loving Father…*' This means that we need to exercise an ascetical spirit which we call the spirit of divine filiation. In order for this to be 'second nature' to us we need to reflect on the supernatural reality which is expressed in Psalm 2: '*filius meus es tu, ego, hodie, genui te*' ('*you are my son I have begotten you this day*'). Then the Psalm goes on to say '*postula a me et dabo gentes haereditatem tuam terminus terrae*' ('ask of me and I will give you the nations for your inheritance'). This means adopting the role of our King Christ and seeking to lay the world of souls at God's feet. When St Josemaría received the basic message of what God wanted of him, when until then he had merely a kind of hunch of what God wanted, it was certainly to spread the call to holiness to all parts of society. Divine filiation equips the soul for this. It enables the person to live unity of life, and so present Christ to others, convert all one's work and activities into a prayer and a divine offering, sanctify everything by uniting it with Christ's Sacrifice through the Mass and converting it into a means of drawing all the world and souls to God.

In practice, this is a tall order, and in order to live it, it needs to be united to that of spiritual childhood. Don Flavio Capucci, who looked after the Cause of Canonisation of St Josemaría and obviously through his work had a deep understanding of St Josemaría's spirit, once said, in my presence, about twenty years ago, that divine filiation belongs to the essence of the spirit of the Work, whereas the spirit of childhood is a matter of choice. He based this on the manner in which St Josemaría had received the inspirations: the former, by direct divine inspiration, the latter through his own deduction if we can call it that, when he learnt from the nuns in the Patronato de Santa Isabel, that they had the quaint custom of allowing the most junior nun in the Convent to become Mother Superior on the day of the Holy Innocents. At this, St Josemaría with his vivid mind, imagined himself in Heaven, totally in charge telling all the august inhabitants what to do as if he were boss. This led him to have an immense confidence in prayer, very ambitious, which revealed itself in Josemaría's own virtues of magnanimity and magnificence, while remembering he was only a tiny little child of no importance: humility. Needless to say, a child full of hope.

HOPE OF BECOMING SAINTS

ST THOMAS AQUINAS SAID THAT if anyone had been told they would lose their soul and be damned, they should reply that they did not believe this because they were full of hope. We are not in Heaven yet but we have a foothold, we already possess heaven, or, if you like, have a hold on it through the virtue of hope. And still, our enemy might argue, God has laid down very strict conditions, the fulfilment of his commandments, and so on. This is true, but when the Angels appeared to the shepherds minding their flock of sheep by night, they sang out: *'Peace on earth to men of good will'*. St Thomas was once asked by his sister how to get into heaven and he said 'Will it'. This means that those people who do not believe in God, will not be able to hope in him. Faith, as it says in the Letter to the Hebrews, is the *'substance of things to be hoped for' (Heb 11:1)*, so the children of God, are always full of joy in anticipation of the happiness of Heaven. This means also that they will continually fight for holiness, with a deep-seated sense of future success. Of course, the spirit of struggle is based on this virtue of hope, which leads us to fight with real determination and with good will. People often talk of others having a strong will. Very often this means that they are very selfish and always want their own way. Our will has to be strong as well as good. What is it to have a good will? For this we need the aid of philosophical thinking. Things are good in themselves. If you say this a good apple, what you are saying is that it is good in itself, sweet to the taste, firm to the touch, in other words, a good apple. Actions, roads, intentions are good according to the direction they take.

Is this the right road to Liverpool (supposing that Liverpool as a thing is good!) if so, we say *'Good'*! This is also true of the will which is our faculty which should seek the good if it is a good will. Now, it is also true that your will is weak. If anyone comes along and says to you, *'Liverpool? I would not go there if I were you'* and you say, *'Oh, all right then, I won't go'*, without any hesitation or argument, clearly your will is practically non-existent. In his guidance of souls, St Josemaría was well aware of this and continually encouraged people to fight, to engage in a serious interior struggle.

Let's read a point or two from *The Way*. Here is point no. 316:

> *'You tell me, yes, that you want to. Very good: but do you want to as a miser longs for gold, as mother loves her child, as a worldling craves for honours, or as a wretched sensualist seeks his pleasure? No? Then, you don't want to'.*

This point, among others, is emphasising the aspect of strength. The following points, 317 and so on do the same, but when it comes to his advice about strengthening a weak will, we have to go back to no. 19:

> *'Will-power. A very important quality. Don't despise little things, for by the continual practice of denying yourself again and again in such things -which are never futile or trivial- with God's grace you will add strength and resilience to you will. In that way you will first become master of yourself, and then a guide, a chief, a leader: to compel and to sway and to inspire others, with your word, with your example, with your knowledge and with your authority'.*

What has he told us here? That we strengthen our will by putting into practice little sacrifices; which for students means tackling studies, (see no. 337), living the heroic minute of getting up on time in the morning.

Now, once we have worked on our will by strengthening it, we have to make sure that it is a 'good' will. Otherwise, what is the point? We would just be joining the enemy once more. There is no shadow of a doubt that the Devil has a mighty will!

This, of course, is where the grace of God comes in. This too, is mentioned in no. 19 where it says, '*with God's grace*'. The grace referred to is God's actual grace, as opposed to sanctifying grace, and this, we must remember, is really the Holy Spirit.

Following a proper sequence, we should be dealing with the Holy Spirit at the end, when we deal with his coming down upon the Apostles at Pentecost. But the Holy Spirit does not confine himself to a particular moment in history, He is, needless to say, with us all the time. Our Lord said '*I will send you another Paraclete*' *(Jn 14:16),* obviously referring to the fact that the Apostles had got used to relying on Jesus all the time. He was their support, he was their strength, their joy and their love. So, when Jesus ascended into Heaven, the Apostles were broken-hearted. They instinctively turned to Mary, as we should do, when we are down. But she consoled them and taught them how to prepare for the Coming of the Holy Spirit, with prayer and in union together with Mary their Mother. We should be doing this ourselves all the time. We should be continually turning to our Mother, with great confidence and trust, so that she will enable us to receive the Holy Spirit, who will bring his gifts and strengthen our will. We notice this in the description of the actual events in the Acts of the Apostles and we become aware how the weak and cowardly Apostles became strong, fiery and outspoken Apostles, just like their Master, who spoke with authority; as no-one else had ever spoken.

I hope with all this about having a strong will, and so on, we do not lose sight of the fact that sanctity - that is, holiness of life, being truly good - is God's work in us. God is bent on making us saints, and what we have to do is be humble, not resist his grace and pray. For it is prayer that allows God to have access to our souls and raise them up to his level. If you think about it rationally, you realise the truth Our Lord was putting across in his analogy about the vine and the branches. Without Him, <u>nothing</u>.

Holiness is sharing in God's life, and God alone can raise us up to his level. Suppose you stop a man riding along a motor-way on a bicycle and you ask him where he is you going. And he replies, 'to the Moon'. 'But you can't get to the moon, on a bicycle' you say, and he treads more heavily on the pedals and says, 'just watch me'! You would take him for a madman. So similarly, we would have to describe a person who tried to reach holiness, the goodness of God, by his own efforts. And yet, this is what we do. Furthermore, the proof of it is that when we fail, having tried our best, we are disappointed and become sad. We are intelligent human beings; we should have realised. Many people of course are a bit short as regards intelligence. They should make sure they read the Sacred Scriptures which tell us this all the time.

SIN AND LUKEWARMNESS

WHEN WE FAIL TO FULFIL our general vocation to holiness, we call it sin. When we fail to fulfil our specific vocation, to what God wants us to do in particular, we call it lukewarmness. Sin is *'praevaricatio legis'* – *'the breaking of the law'*, which may be, as we saw before, God's direct law, the ten commandments, or God's indirect law, enunciated by the Church or the State, the two perfect societies which can make laws. St Augustine gave us another definition, which fits in much better with what we saw when discussing Eve's transgression - original sin. This is *'aversio a Deo et conversio ad creaturas'* – *'a turning away from God, and turning towards creatures'*.

It is always advisable to spend some time, unless we suffer from scruples making a good examination of conscience. There are books aplenty which provide appropriate questions, so this is not the place, but it is nevertheless useful to run over the ten commandments and our duties of state, which make up or include, in some cases the vocation to which we have been called by God. St Francis de Sales, gave us a very good rule of thumb which is valid for all states of life, namely that the measure of our love of God is given by our hatred for sin. So, this means, we are looking for the measure of our detestation of sin. When we come to die, a key factor is our detachment from sin. There was a film produced some years ago which I did not see, but which I think was called 'Fatal Attraction'. If a soul is fatally attached to some sin, that is to say, a sin or vice they cannot bring themselves to reject, then they cannot enter Heaven, and when we come to die, we cannot change. As the expression goes in the gambling world, the die is cast. In the Sacred Scripture, somewhere, it says: *'as the tree falls, so will it lie' (Eccles 11:3).*

When, on the other hand, we look at lukewarmness, we suffer from another kind of fatal attachment, which is to venial sin. What is meant by venial sin, as opposed to mortal sin is as the name itself indicates. Mortal sin, is taken from the Latin *mors/ mortis* that is, death. Venial sin is taken from the Latin, *venia/veniae* pardon, permission or forgiveness, in other words, a pardonable sin. Now it is because the sin is relatively small, less grave, and can be forgiven by an act of contrition or some sacramental like using holy water or receiving a priest's blessing, people unfortunately pay less attention to committing it. Here, in Thornycroft Hall (where I am writing this book), on the Feast of St Bartholomew 1980, Blessed Alvaro, was asked a question by one of the people attending the large get-together outside the Annexe of this building and it was *'What did St Josemaría mean when he said* **'enter into the wound of Our Lord's side'**? And without any hesitation, Blessed Alvaro replied: *'Imagine Our Lord's heart being pricked by thorns. Do we not realise how it would pain him? Well, this is what our venial sins do to Jesus'*. This has given me food for thought over the years. It should give all of us the desire to avoid all venial sins at whatever cost! When, however, we are lukewarm we get into the habit of committing many venial sins, saying to ourselves - well, it is only a venial sin, I won't go to Hell because of it, forgetting that it is an offence against God, and great cause of suffering to Our Lord Jesus Christ.

When I mentioned earlier that there was a fatal attachment to venial sin, I meant that there was no effort at all to stop committing these venial sins. We treat them as if they did not count at all. The reason is, quite frequently, we have got into the habit and this is a consequence of some vice we have acquired over the years. It follows from our predominant defect which is a tendency which takes its root from the consequence of original sin: irascibility or concupiscence. When someone, possibly in our close family, says or does something we take exception to, we utter a sharp word, or even a swear word, and we don't see the need to apologise. And if we are told, to keep a better guard over these injurious words, we say, *'Oh, I have always been like this so you will just have to put up with it'*. Or again, if something pops up on the television, or the Internet which is clearly against holy purity and we give in to curiosity, we say as an excuse, *'It is the way I am, I have always been like this, it is the way I have been made' (cf. The Way no. 4)*, thereby indirectly putting the blame on God! In this case, one of two things will take place if we don't do anything about it. One, in the extreme case, the venial sins lead us into mortal sin, and with same attitude of a fatal attraction, on the day of judgement we are found wanting. Do you remember the words of the master when he came to the servant who had buried his talent: *'You unfaithful and lazy servant!' (Mt 25:26).* He was condemned for his laziness, which was in reality his unwillingness to fulfil his master's commission. Or, in the less extreme case, he will spend a great deal of time in purgatory until the habit or vice is completely purified.

From this we can deduce the importance of the general examination of conscience, which St Josemaría suggests on days of retreat, and also of discovering what is our besetting fault, or dominant defect, and then, once isolated, making it the subject of a particular examination of conscience and then over a period of time fighting to eliminate it.

Lukewarmness as we know, is not confined to venial sin. In the Apocalypse, when the Angels of the various Churches are addressed (by the way in this passage it is clear that Angel stands for Bishop), the Church at Ephesus is commended for several good things - little patience with wickedness, etc. but then reprimanded:

'Yet there is one charge I make against thee; of losing the charity that was thine at first' (Rv 2:4). In other words, lukewarmness is basically the loss of the love of God. This is because love is a dynamic virtue; it cannot stay still. It is a fire, which, if not fed with more combustible fuel will die out. Without prayer, our charity will fade away. Furthermore, it grows with the acts of charity we make as time goes by.

Our Lord's parable of the Good Samaritan says it all. When we are lukewarm, we fail to see the distress of those around us, we don't see their needs; or if we do, we pass by on the other side, perhaps with the excuse that we haven't got the time.

I have not been to Palestine, but I understand that when Our Lord, said the priest and the Levite went <u>down</u> from Jerusalem to Jericho, he meant down, and someone pointed out to me, the priest and the Levite had finished their work in Jerusalem, and were on their way home so they had plenty of time to perform that work of service which the Good Samaritan did. So, this is another big area for examination of conscience.

Insights

And we must bear in mind that laziness, in the spiritual life, finds its expression in sloth: one of the seven capital sins. In his book '*The Ladder of Perfection*', St John Climacus describes sloth as insensibility of heart. With it the mind and soul adopt a peculiar ability to be at variance with each other. There is an inbuilt spirit of contradiction continually at work. For example, the man who talks about the importance of temperance and proceeds to eat more than before; the preacher who extols the value of silence and talks at tiresome length about that virtue, which is the enemy of long speeches; He exhorts others to meekness, and in the very midst of his exhortations frequently gives way to bitterness and sarcasm. Obviously, sloth is the sworn enemy of examination of conscience, for it seems that the making of a resolution is the surest guarantee that no steps with be taken to correct the fault that has been discovered. Pride, another capital sin, is clearly at the bottom of this strange tendency, for it is not laziness, pure and simple, but laziness in the spiritual struggle, almost an aversion towards conversion. When I read the chapter relating to this in St John's classical work, he said that there were many causes of sloth, and was not clear about how to solve the problem. This is telling us how difficult it is to combat sloth and with it, lukewarmness.

Without claiming to have one simple solution to this problem, it is abundantly clear that it has to be a supernatural solution. Lukewarmness is a human thing. It is the equivalent of the possessed boy encountered by the disciples when Our Lord was up the mountain and transfigured in front of St Peter, St James and St John *(cf. Matt 17:18)*.

The disciples could not cast out the unclean spirit; they asked Our Lord, and he performs the miracle, but then he adds '*there is no way of casting out such spirits as this except by prayer and fasting*' *(Mt 17:21)*. As far as I can make out, the reason Our Lord says this is because when we have recourse to prayer and fasting in a spirit of faith, we facilitate the working of the Holy Spirit; He is able to grant the soul his precious gifts, and especially the fire of his love. He promises this via the Prophet Ezechiel: '*Will you doubt, then, the Lord's power, when I open your graves and revive you? When I breathe my spirit into you, to give you life again, and dwell at peace in your own land*? *(Ez 37:4)*. Now, this fits in very well with one of the promises made by Our Lord to St Margaret Mary - that devotion to the Sacred Heart, which we know is about Our Lord's Eucharist Heart being on fire, would mean: <u>tepid souls will</u> <u>become fervent.</u> And I think we can add to that, by following St Josemaría's advice in *The Way*, no. 492: *'Love for our Mother will be the breath that kindles into a living flame the embers of virtue hidden in the ashes of your indifference.'* Clearly, a new conversion is needed. Don Alvaro calls lukewarmness a *'disease of the will'*. This needs to be set on fire once more. As we pray can we not look back to when we first felt the warmth of the touches of the Paraclete and first fell in love with God?

CONFESSION

ACCORDING TO ST FRANCIS DE Sales, correspondence to the inspirations of the Holy Spirit can be compared with the proposal of a young man to his girlfriend, asking her hand in marriage. Three steps are required: one, the suitor's proposal, then the lady's consideration of the proposal and then her consent. Obviously he says, if the suitor courted the lady for a long time and she refused even to consider his proposal, he would be offended. To take pleasure in inspirations disposes us to give glory to God and pleases him, for although it is not the same as consent it leads to it. So, it is a good sign to take pleasure in listening to the word of God, and St Francis quotes the Canticle of Canticles 5:6 where it says: '*How my heart melted at the sound of his voice*'. Something similar can apply to Confession. What we do not appreciate sufficiently, in my opinion, is that the proposal to go to Confession, is an inspiration of the Holy Spirit. Certainly, the perfect reception of the Sacrament, is a tremendous source of grace and has the power of transforming our life and soul. It is, or should be, the object of hope, where we trust that God will grant us grace and glory. Priests should all be aware of this and how they are performing God's work when they offer this Sacrament to the faithful. However, let us return to the thoughts we were considering earlier. When we entertain the thought of making our Confession which involves making an act of true repentance, combined with a firm resolution to amend our ways, we obviously please Almighty God. Our Father God is delighted. In the same way, as in the Parable of the Prodigal Son, the Father saw his son coming from a distance, and appreciated that he had already entertained in his heart the reunion with his father and the total rejection of his wicked ways, for all that was now needed was to throw himself into his father's arms. So it is when we go to Confession. We need to make that consideration of blessings and graces, which we anticipate on receiving absolution, forgiveness and mercy of our Father-God. In saying all this and adapting St Francis de Sales' analogy, I am aware, that comparing Confession with Marriage is stretching things a little, for as we know, Marriage is definitive and Confession, strictly speaking is not. However, I am unrepentant, because it is high time as penitents we took the Sacrament of Reconciliation or Confession more seriously and that we be totally resolved to abandon our evil ways. Unfortunately, these days, how often we hear people say... I will *try not* to sin again, when they should be saying I *will not* sin again. We have to make a firm purpose of amendment.

PREDOMINANT DEFECT

We all have a predominant defect or besetting fault. This is often the cause of our repeated sins, usually venial but not necessarily venial. Some people repeatedly commit mortal sins for the same reason: a deep-seated inclination to sensuality or impurity. Another person may be afflicted with greed, or inclined to lose his temper at the slightest provocation. The first thing to do is to identify it. Unfortunately, pride often comes in to blind us and you quite frequently find people who are totally convinced that either the fault is minimal or even non-existent. I think I have found a way of finding out what it is that afflicts us. First of all, you have to try and work out what you consider to be your strongest asset. Good, I am usually very quiet and serene I rarely lose my temper, I am quite patient when provoked and when other people I know would get very angry indeed. If this is the case, I think you will find you are too easy-going and I might even say, bone idle. Another person might say I like to get things done, I am an active dynamic person, as a rule. I might even say I share St Paul's drive and apostolic enthusiasm. Well, if we look into things a bit more calmly and humbly, we might find, we share in Saul's cruel attitude before his conversion, and find we don't suffer fools gladly, and are quite impatient with slow-coaches, and people who dither. So, you see, when you identify your assets you find this is also a source of some failing. So, then, once you have identified your predominant fault, you speak to your spiritual director or counsellor, and suggest a particular examination which is adapted to eliminating the said defect. I was filled with admiration for St Josemaría for he always seemed to have an answer for most spiritual problems. So, for example, he would say things like: '*problemas de genio, son problemas de piedad*' which means if you have got a bad temper then the way to solve it is examine your spirit of piety: say more aspirations, more acts of love, have a greater devotion to the Holy Eucharist. Keep good presence of God and then you won't be inclined to jump to conclusions and avoid a violent human reaction. With that example I have opted for an easy solution. But such is the richness of St Josemaría's ascetical wisdom, I am sure we can confidently assert as he did, referring to the Church's spiritual treasury: we have all the medicine (*toda la farmacopea*) to cure our faults. Nevertheless, it has to be said that the essential element is to fight for sanctity or we will not get anywhere.

GENERAL CONFESSION

It is always a good idea on a retreat, especially since we only do them once a year, to make a general Confession. When St Josemaría did his retreat in Segovia, (I think it was in the Carmelite Convent), one of the priests said to him, shall I give you some talks? he replied, 'No, thank you, I would just like to go to Confession at the end'. Obviously, if you are really alone you might find going to Confession somewhat difficult, so it is up to your own ingenuity as to how to solve this problem. You can either go to your own Parish Priest, or, alternatively your spiritual director. In any event, I am proposing that you take special care in making a general examination. If, however, it should be the case that you are scrupulous, I would not recommend making a general examination. The thing is that nowadays we tend to find that most people don't suffer from scruples, but rather tend to be too easy-going and lax. There are several ways to carry out this examination of conscience. I have come across several booklets which list plenty of questions, and I have no quarrel with that, but my personal feeling is that you make a general examination best of all if you treat it as prayer, that is to say, a personal intimate conversation with Our Lord. To begin with you pray to the Holy Spirit, for he is the one who is going to enlighten you, and he is the spirit of truth. You need to ask very earnestly for the virtue of humility because humility is the virtue which lets us know how we stand before God. The big problem we all have to face is that in identifying sins we tend to be creatures of habit and come up with the same old faults. How many people will say, I have tailed off in making frequent Confession because I got tired of saying the same things? But why is this, if not because we examine ourselves in a sense independently of God. We have to be sorry not for the way we think something is offensive to God, but what he considers is a sin and offensive to him. And how do we know this? The short answer is to say by Divine Revelation. One of the main subjects we have to study in Dogmatic Theology is Revelation, and when asked, 'what is that'? again, the short answer is the *locutio Dei* the speech or word of God. What God has said. However, in this place, this is what has God said, what he wants us to do, and what he does not. Nowadays, there is a grave danger of falling into relativism, some kind of situation ethics, where people make their own minds up about what is a sin and what is not. People shy away from the truth; pride gets in the way and prevents us from admitting what is sometimes grossly offensive to God. In other words, following the first paragraph to the Hebrews, where it says *'God spoke in many ways, first through the Prophets, and then through his Son'* (Heb 1:1). We go through the Commandments and then through the Gospel. Undoubtedly, quite a number of people reading this will complain: 'But how can I work out from the Sacred Scripture the meaning of the Ten Commandments, and learn from the Gospel, what was pleasing or displeasing to Christ'? The answer to that query is to get hold of a good Catechism like that produced by Archbishop Sheehan and brought up to date recently, and go through the section that refers to the Commandments. As regards the procedure, which I hinted at earlier, doing our examination of conscience is like an intimate prayer. You say, is there any way, my Lord, in which I have offended you, this day, this week, or this year. Mary, my Mother, help me to discover what you find in my life is displeasing to your Son, Jesus etc.

THE LAST THINGS

THE GASPARRI CATECHISM, CHAPTER XII has the title '*The Last Things*', and he starts it off with question 580: *What very effective means for avoiding sin does God recommend to us in Holy Scripture?*

In Holy Scripture God recommends to us a very effective means for avoiding sin, when he bids us reflect on the Last Things: '*In all thy works remember thy last end and thou shalt never sin*' (Sir 7:40)

The Latin quotation from Sirach is '*in operibus tuis memorare finem tuum et in aeternum non peccabis*' which actually says, '*you will not sin eternally*'. This, of course, is considerably different from the given translation, which, we have to admit despite this, is helpful. The given translation is saying it deters us from committing sin; my translation is saying that remembering your final end will stop you from committing sin that will take you into Hell. Of course, we don't want to commit sin of any kind, but above all it is essential to avoid damnation! Nowadays, you find in society people don't seem to believe in any Afterlife. They seem to think that when you come to die, that is the end not just of life but of existence. Our Lord, however, in the Holy Gospel is very clear: '*What does it profit a man to gain the whole world and suffer the loss of his own soul*'? *(Mk 8:36)*. Translations lose the force of this by saying 'life' instead of soul. There is a vast difference, not just in the meaning of the words, but the significance. To lose one's soul is of course to be damned. The expression to save one's soul means to go to Heaven, and to lose it to go to Hell. But going back to Our Lord's words, he wants us to realise that, beautiful as the world is, with its many precious things, and experiences and memories for many people, none of it is in any way comparable with spending eternity with God.

Once again, we have to bring back to our notice that we do not know God; we simply must not put this world on a par with God. It is always helpful, to recall the words of *The Way*, no. 432: '*Consider what is most beautiful and most noble on earth, what pleases the mind and the other faculties, and what delights the flesh and the senses. And the world, and the other worlds that shine in the night: the whole universe.*

Well this, along with all the follies of the heart satisfied, is worth nothing, is less and less than nothing, compared ... with this God of mine! - of yours! Infinite treasure, pearl of great price, humbled, become a slave, reduced to the form of a servant in the stable where he chose to be born, in Joseph's workshop, in his passion and in his ignominious death... and in the madness of Love which is the blessed Eucharist.'

It is saying, in effect, how can you possibly throw away your destiny to live out your eternal existence, separated from God, and suffering in Hell. '*The fool has said in his heart, there is no God*' (Ps 14:1). To use our freedom to choose this world and its pleasures and comforts, for the few years of life, instead of God, who made the world and all that is in it, is just madness. The point in *The Way* just quoted, helps us to realise the burning love of God for each one of us. However, to get back to the words of the Catechism. What it is really saying is what many Saints have advised us to do in order to be able to live a healthy spiritual life - meditate on the Last Things from time to time, at least once a month.

But what are these Last Things? Generally, people say just the four: Death, Judgment, Hell and Heaven. Even in listing them, Purgatory is omitted; we know it does not go on forever, but it does exist and we can say that, overall, most Catholics go to Purgatory. This is in itself justification for its inclusion. Its inclusion is rejected by Protestants as we know, but the discussion will have to wait until we have dealt with death.

DEATH

IN THE HOLY GOSPEL, OUR Lord seems reluctant to speak about death, in the way we do, as the termination of our life on earth and the separation of the soul and the body.

He talks about sleep. When he raises the daughter of Jairus back to life he says she is sleeping, they laugh him to scorn because she really is dead, as we know it, then he goes and brings her back to life; he does the same thing with Lazarus, and says he is going to awaken him from his sleep. When the disciples take him literally, he clarifies that Lazarus is truly dead, and, indeed he has been so for four days! When we read the Apocalypse, we see why Our Lord does this. It is to distinguish it from the second death, which is to be lost in Hell. Now the death we are talking about is the first death. This is where the soul and the body are separated from each other. Life on earth is over, the time allotted to us for meriting graces and Heaven itself has run out. The time given to man to work out his eternal salvation varies from person to person. Some people live quite a long time compared to others, some, a short time. This is determined by God. Certain circumstances prevailing on earth may make the time a person given by God, is curtailed, by disease, or violence as during a war. This, we would have to say, in consideration of the fact that it is a great grace and privilege given to us by God to merit heaven, is grave misfortune, and why war is a great scourge, shortening a man's opportunity to serve God and earn his salvation.

There is a very enlightening homily by St Josemaría, to be found in *'Friends of God'* (a collection of homilies), entitled *'Time is a Treasure'*. From time to time, and particularly once, I remember, he used to repeat a phrase taken from St Paul: *'tempus breve est' (Time is short)*. This became a kind of watchword for him, as it can be for us. Time is short. We have to make the most of it. There is another very telling point in *The Way* which is relevant to our subject, no. 355:

> 'Those who are engaged in business say that time is money. That seems little to me: for us who are engaged in affairs of souls, time is glory!'

This is telling us to make the most of our time. This means of course, not just filling it or, or worse still, killing it, as people say. As St Josemaría states, we have to give all the glory to God, this entails, keeping in God's presence and offering everything to him with purity of intention. St Paul says to the Ephesians

> 'Look carefully then how you walk, not as unwise men but as wise making the most of the time, because the days are evil. Therefore, do not be foolish, but understand what the will of the Lord is' (Eph 5:15).

What does it mean 'to make the most of time'? As always, it is to see things from God's point of view, to understand what He wants from us and then to use all the talents he has given us and to make the most of them. Did the man who went off on his travels and give to his servant the talents not say to them *'Negotiamini dum venio'*? *('Trade with these until I return') (Lk 19:13)*. For along with the money, he granted them the time and opportunity to make a profit. And when he came back, he expected to see a profit. One of the servants buried his talent in a hole in the ground instead of trading with his talent and making a profit, but the other two doubled the amount of money they had been given. Now what kind of profit did God have in mind? Obviously supernatural fruit, acts of charity, works of apostolate leading to conversions and correspondence to grace. The Council of Trent says that when we die and present ourselves before the Tribunal of Christ, we have to show him the deeds of our body whether good or ill, nor is there left for anyone any more time for repentance. This means that when we come to die, the die is cast, the time of merit is over and done with. During our lifetime we can ask for forgiveness for the evil things we have done and the good things we have omitted. This shows us the value of making a good examination of conscience at the end of each day to see how we have spent the day - giving glory to God or just pandering to our selfish pleasures and enjoyment.

In one of his beautiful sermons St Bernard says love is all that really matters and that this is expressed in fulfilling God's will. We can ask ourselves 'have I served God with true love, with rectitude of intention'? because we know that very often, we do things for our own satisfaction instead of for God's glory. It is for this reason we should submit ourselves to some kind of plan of life. This is to establish some key elements of piety through the day. We should attend Holy Mass, every day if possible, do some time of prayer, by which I mean mental prayer, the Holy Rosary, the recitation of the Angelus at least at noon, a time of spiritual reading, never forgetting to include a few minutes of the Holy Gospel. Do you remember Joseph of the coat of many colours and how it is described in the Old Testament that he won the Egyptian Pharaoh's favour by interpreting his dreams? Well, we have the dream of the seven fat cows and then the seven thin ones. This was as interpreted as that there would be seven years of plenty, and seven years of famine. In the spiritual life it means that we should make sure that when things are going well for us, we are calm and serene, not subject to severe temptations, we should fulfil the norms of our plan of life, with love and attention, deriving all the benefit and grace God has to bestow. So, we are then prepared for more difficult times, and we have the supernatural strength to withstand the onslaught of great temptations. In the same way, we should take great care to do our work calmly and serenely like Joseph, the most chaste spouse of the Blessed Virgin Mary. It has to be obvious to everyone that St Joseph, our Father and Lord, was never at a loss. All of a sudden, he was commanded by the Angel to get up and go to Egypt to protect the Child and his Mother, and he was able to get up on the spot and obey God's holy will, because he was already prepared. Oh, that we could do the same! Well we can if we are similarly provident, and make the most of the graces we receive every day. One of the ways this is expressed in St Josemaría's writings is when he refers to everyday work. In *The Way* no. 373 he writes: '*I like your apostolic motto: Work without resting*'.

Another way of ensuring we do not waste our precious time is to make sure we exercise the virtue of charity. This is not surprising when we realise that it is the love in our hearts that God is seeking. We remember the saying of the Old Testament: *'Da fili mi, cor tuum mihi'* (*'My son, give me your heart!'*) (Proverbs 23:26).

And so, all our good deeds of charity towards our neighbour are so many acts of love towards God, because he takes all the good works we perform as so many signs of love towards him. Furthermore, all our acts of charity help other souls in their progress towards God and are an integral part of God's universal plan of salvation.

That is why when we are making most of our time we are really responding to the promptings of the Holy Spirit, who breathes where he will. I remember when St Josemaría died, we had a visit from Don Ernesto Julia, who worked very closely with him, right up to the time of his death. And Don Ernesto said, as a kind of spontaneous positive witness to the Father's sanctity: *'El Padre no perdía ni una'* *'The Father never missed a single opportunity'*. For example, if anything required repair, or something had to be put back on the shelf, St Josemaría would not hesitate to do it. If he could not attend to it there and then, he would make a note to have it done as soon as possible. Speaking about making the most of time and of St Josemaría will, of course, bring to mind that for most of his life he did not wear a watch. Apart from a sign of detachment, this was also a way of showing that his philosophy of life was first of all, just to do God's will as indicated by his two appointed assistants Don Alvaro or Don Javier as an act of obedience, and also, doing one thing after another, making the most of time.

Clearly, all of this demands great self-discipline, a lot of practice, and being alert all the time. Being alert was clearly one of our Blessed Mother's qualities as she demonstrated at the wedding feast of Cana in Galilee. She noticed that the wine was running out, and in addition supplied the remedy for what would be a disaster for the young newly-weds.

Finally, the Old Testament has some very apt observations to make concerning the kind of person who is inclined to sit back and waste time. The Old Testament says:

> '*Slothfulness casts into a deep sleep and an idle soul shall suffer hunger. Because of the cold, the sluggard would not plough; he shall beg, therefore, in the summer and it shall not be given him. He that observes the wind does not sow, and he that considers the clouds does not reap*' (Proverbs 19:15).

Then we have St Gregory the Great who advises the hasty:

'*My son do thou nothing without counsel and thou shalt not repent when thou hast done: let thy eyelids go before thy steps*'. This saying may have prompted St Josemaría to warn us against 'journeys of laziness'. This is when, through hurrying too much, we run upstairs to get a book, then when we get down to our desk, we find we have forgotten a dictionary or some other item we would have remembered had we not been so hasty. This is called precipitancy if we want to use the right word, but it is really just thoughtlessness.

Again, this brings St Joseph to mind once more. He was never at a loss, because he was calm and serene. In fact, we have the feeling that if we had had the privilege of being with Jesus, Mary and Joseph we would have sensed a great feeling of peace and serenity. St Josemaría taught us that in order to reach the Trinity of Heaven we should cultivate intimacy with the Trinity on Earth. One of the reasons being, that in both Trinities we breathe the sweet air of peace. From these words, it could be suggested we have already arrived in Heaven. Well, we are still a long way off: after Death comes the Judgement.

JUDGMENT

'It has been established for men to die once, and after this the judgment' (Heb 9:27).

WHAT A TREMENDOUS EVENT TO look forward to, to meet up with Christ on the judgment seat. It is said that when one comes to die, one sees exactly what one deserves and where one has to go. Generally, it is accepted that the majority of people, or, at least Catholics, will go to Purgatory. This is not difficult to imagine when you stop to think about the absolute holiness and purity of God. Now it is highly unlikely that one is pure enough, or holy enough to go straight into Heaven. Frank Sheed says in his little book, *'Theology for Beginners'*, that there is one question we must ask when someone comes to die and that is, is this soul in a state of grace or not? For if you are in a state of grace, then to Heaven you can go, because you have the power to live there. But if you are not in the state of grace, then your place is in Hell. Of course, being in a state of grace does not, of itself, qualify you for entry in Heaven straightaway. What it means is that with the appropriate purification, you will be able to enter Heaven, because, by being in a state of grace you will be able to receive the Beatific Vision which will give you the ability to contemplate God, face to face. So, at this particular judgment, as it is commonly called, the soul sees itself, as it is before God and throws itself into the fires of purgatory to be purified. Most authors are agreed, although this is not defined doctrine, but based on the revelations of St Bede's History of the English people, that there are two levels of Purgatory. For souls that have just scraped through the examination of the particular judgment, because they have lived a life remote from God, and finally said they were sorry to Him, and managed to receive the last anointing, they will have to go to the part of purgatory nearest to Hell and suffer a great deal for a long space of time. But souls who gave their lives, working for God, cultivating a spiritual life of faithfulness to God to the best of their ability, and yet committed a few venial sins, or were neglectful in their duties, will enter into a kind of waiting room, where the principal pain is the privation of the Beatific Vision. Some souls, I am told but I do not know how true it is, that those who have committed quite a lot of sins and made a deathbed repentance are not allowed to be helped by the suffrages of the faithful on earth. Those in the waiting room can and are helped by the prayers, sacrifices and the Masses said for them.

But what about the General Judgment? I was under the impression, you say, that the Judgment took place at the end of the world, with everybody in the Valley of Jehosaphat? Indeed, this is so. But why have two judgments? It's bad enough having one. The answer is very simple. It is on account of the discrepancy of time, between when you die, and the end of the world. Half of us will be judged during the lifetime of the earth, the other half on the Day of Judgment. Did you realise that at any given moment, the number of souls who have passed away is roughly equal to those still alive? It is a curious mathematical phenomenon. So those who died before will join up with those who have not yet been judged. But how will we all fit into the valley? There are two possible answers to this conundrum. One is that the Valley is whatever size is required to accommodate the whole human race, for after all, Jehosaphat only means Judgment anyway. The other, should we say, more theological explanation comes from St Thomas who has an answer for practically everything. He says, in his book about the Creed, that not everybody will be there. Take Our Lady, for example, how is it possible for her to undergo any judgment in view of her privileged position? The same would apply to St Joseph and St John the Baptist, who, we could say, never put a foot wrong. Then St Thomas says, the twelve Apostles will not be judged because the opposite is true, for they will judge the twelve tribes of Israel. Then, and this is the master stroke, there is a vast multitude of people who will not be judged, because they have been judged already. These are those souls who when confronted with Jesus Christ Our Lord, refused to acknowledge Him and, unfortunately, are already condemned. How many they are, I would hesitate to guess, but seemingly it would, unfortunately be very many!

Against this rather depressing observation, we have a beautiful testimony of Bishop Thomas Holland, in his autobiography, where he describes how in his ministry as troop chaplain in the D-Day landings, as he went from ship to ship where the wounded and the dying, were looked after, he gave the dying the crucifix to kiss, and out of all the hundreds of wounded he attended to, only one turned aside. We know and believe in the wonderful mercy of God. Perhaps many of these young men might well have to spend a long period in purgatory, but thanks to God's mercy and the generosity of a saintly priest, they were saved at the eleventh hour.

But, at this stage, you might quite well say, you still have not answered the original question; why have another judgment, after you know the fate of the individual person as given in the particular judgment? The answer is justice. Justice not only has to be done, but be seen to be done. The general judgment, takes account of the series of consequences, that follow on from the lives of each person. We men are not isolated units, which have no effect on those around us; our actions often have a very serious and long-lasting influence on our contemporaries and successors. Just think of the good that the holy Curé of Ars had on his parishioners and on the thousands of good souls who trouped to his Confessional. Then, again, think of all those holy priests who in later years have been influenced by his wonderful example.

I am not sure whether it was a child or an adult, who, in some sort of supernatural guise said to him, as if it were the Devil who was speaking: if there were four more like you, my kingdom would be at an end! Well, while we have tried to put across the argument of the influence of good example on the lives of others, it does appear, unfortunately, that these other four have not turned up, if we are to judge by the sorry state of the present affairs in the Church and in the world. Then we have to consider the effect of bad behaviour and example, following the lives of the miscreants. On retreats, I have preached in the past, I used to make what at least I thought was a humorous observation, suggesting

Mrs Hitler, might well be heard to exclaim, well I don't know, whatever happened to our Adolf, I gave him everything he ever wanted! What a contrast with St Monica, the mother of St Augustine. I believe it was St Ambrose who was reported to have said: a son of so many tears, cannot be lost! So it is that the lives of the just are followed by many good works and lives of other holy people, and similarly, the lives of those who have behaved badly are followed by many disastrous consequences, which cannot be fully assessed until the Final Judgment. So that is why we need a second Judgment at the end of the world.

Now, what is the use of our meditation on the event of our judgment by Almighty God?

My idea, which I probably picked up from another preacher, is the parallel which can be made with what used be called 'mock' exams taking place in schools around January or at least after Christmas, where the students took the examinations devised by their own schoolteacher which would simulate as far as possible the real thing in the Summer when their future career would be at stake. The experience of the mock GCSE would prepare them for the later real test. So, this means, that in our spiritual life we should examine our conscience at least once a day, to test our love of God, and how we are striving to live our ascetical struggle. I remember, long ago, 1960 it would be, we had a meditation from St Josemaría in which he almost shouted out: '*examination of conscience, most important, never leave it out*'!

Finally, in the book, '*Immersed in God*', which is an interview with Blessed Alvaro about St Josemaría, halfway through there is a whole examination of conscience written out in 1932 and Don Alvaro makes the shrewd observation that most of the questions St Josemaría put to himself were about his interior struggle, and he also took account of his omissions. If we read chapter 25 of St Matthew's Gospel, there we find Our Lord's own questions that he will ask on the Day of Judgment. And what do we find? Well, that Our Lord asks us did we feed the hungry, give drink to the thirsty, visit the imprisoned? And because we did not, he sends us the same way as the Devil and his Angels. Because you didn't, because you omitted these good deeds, you are condemned. One of the great changes in the New Order of Mass is the Confiteor and it includes sorrow for the omissions. I always think this has special relevance for the Priest, for he is a man who has the great privilege of being able to administer the Sacraments. So, this is what a good priest should examine himself about. Has he celebrated the Sacraments for the people, beginning with the Holy Mass, then being available for Confession, visited the dying and administered the Anointing of the Sick. This is what he was ordained to do: make use of the great spiritual power he has been given by God. He is another Christ, who *'went about doing good' (Acts 10:38).*

PURGATORY

ACCORDING TO MOST AUTHORS THE majority of people go to Purgatory when they die. Of course, nowadays you get a lot of prophets of doom, who predict that most people go to Hell. But God did not create us to send us to Hell and it was about just one individual that Our Lord said, it was '*better for that man if he had not been born*' (Mt 26:24), so he wants us all in Heaven and he is bent on our sanctification and salvation. St Paul says he wants all men to be saved. We must believe God Our Lord and Saviour is doing everything possible for men to reach eternal salvation, as Pope Francis says in his book '*God's name is Mercy*'. However, it may well be true that in order for this to happen, lots of people only just manage to do this at the very last moment of life, which means that they have not made sufficient atonement for their many and grievous sins. There are literally thousands of souls in Purgatory. Many will have to spend a very long time there. I remember being very shocked on reading the story of Our Lady's conversation with Lucia of Fatima. She asked Our Lady about the fate of a number of children who had recently died, one was a girl, … she's gone to Heaven, and another a little boy… Oh he's in Heaven, and what about Amelia? She's in Purgatory till the end of the world! Good Heavens! She was nineteen years of age. This has got to make us think, when we look at our sorry lives! We have spent more than nineteen years on this earth!

The Protestants do not believe in Purgatory. This is a grave omission of true doctrine for which Martin Luther, Zwingli, and John Calvin are responsible. The latter added to this the doctrine of Predestination which is another grave error and similarly damages the belief in the justice of God. However can God be a just God if he predestines half the population to Hell without their having any say in the matter?

He would be grossly unfair as well as denying human freedom. Supposing I were fortunate enough to be included in the ones predestined for Heaven? I would be extremely uncomfortable in contemplating the fate of the damned. I would be saying to myself, 'why them and not me'? 'What have I done to deserve this'? Any concept of merit is also lost. No! This elimination of purgatory is a gross distortion of good doctrine and a grave insult to God. So, then we ask, but how did it come about?

The obvious answer is the one that Luther himself puts forward. He confused original sin with its consequences. I now quote Ludwig Ott:

> 'Original Sin does not consist, as the Reformers, the Baians, and the Jansenists taught, in : The habitual concupiscence, which remains, even in the baptised, a true and proper sin, and that the concupiscence which remains behind after Baptism for the moral proving is called sin in an improper sense only' (Denziger 792).

Every time Luther comes across some evidence of the consequences of original sin for example, sensuality, he concludes we are still in sin, and that, therefore original sin has not been eliminated by Baptism. What the Catholic Church says, however, is that Baptism does remove the sin, and gives the soul sanctifying grace, but leaving man in the weakened state with concupiscence, irascibility, vulnerability, mortality etc. These consequences are left, as quoted above, 'for the moral proving'.

So then what does Luther himself conclude, now that he has declared Baptism to be ineffectual? Well simply that it is faith alone that saves us. He believes that Christ, with his Death, has absorbed the wrath of God, acting, so-to-speak, as a protecting cloak. In fact, he used the scriptural analogy of the scape-goat, explained in Leviticus 16:10 where of two goats, one is chosen by lot to carry the burden of their faults.

This means of course, that, according to Luther, Our Lord's sacrifice of his dead on the Cross, is the whole work of redemption. The matter of Our Lord's wondrous resurrection from the death is a matter of indifference, for the work of redemption is accomplished simply by his death on the Cross. Then you will find the Protestants will claim, 'but did not Christ say this himself, as he was about to die, *consummatum est*; it is accomplished?' But in answer to this we have the words of the first Preface of Easter where it says:

He is the true Lamb who has taken away the sins of the world, for *by dying he has destroyed our death, (that is our supernatural death through sin) and by rising again he has given us new life (Acclamation after the Consecration)*. This then is our life: the life of Christ in our soul. Luther, I understand, was a tormented soul. Even though he went to Confession frequently in his early days, he was not clear in his mind if he was in a state of grace or not, and when he was afflicted with his tendency to sensuality, he saw this as not just a consequence of original sin, but sin itself. To what purpose Baptism, then, or Confession? He says to himself. I am not an unusual person, all this must apply to everybody, and he drew the false conclusion that Baptism was only a sign that Christ was protecting us from the wrath of God. But in order to be sure of this, we need faith. This has another logical conclusion and that is, our good deeds or bad deeds, for that matter, have no effect. Faith and faith alone, matters. The Catholic would argue, 'but what about the Epistle of St James, where it says, faith without works is useless'? 'Bah'! he answers; an Epistle of straw (he was heard to say). Furthermore, since the Resurrection of Christ has been written off, having no effect on our salvation, whether it actually occurred or not is a matter of indifference. And you find that Anglican divines in fact dispute the fact of the Resurrection. And since this is the principal argument for Christ's divinity, most Protestants do not believe that Christ was God. I remember talking to a fellow student when we were on vacation training in Hartlepool working on some filters, and we discussed the divinity of Christ, eventually I said to him, do you believe that Jesus Christ was God? And he replied, not God, the son of God. He could not bring himself to accept the divinity of Christ. He was a Methodist, and quite well versed in religious knowledge, but, like the majority of Protestants, did not believe in the divinity of Christ. St John Henry Newman, in one of his sermons to Mixed Congregations, declared openly, 'Why do most Protestants reject the divinity of Christ?' And answering his own rhetorical question, said, 'because they do not believe in Our Lady' (or similar words). The reason, of course, is because Our Lady knew as no-one else knew, how Our Lord had been born through the working of the Holy Spirit, and therefore was divine. And if Our Lord is God, then she is the Mother of God! Mary is the protectress of Jesus Christ and his identity. No-one knows Jesus Christ better; no-one can lead us to Christ more surely.

Returning to the theme of Purgatory, which is where we started out, I remember reading a short extract from Fr Bede Jarrett, a well-known Dominican, before the war, and he declared that with the denial or Purgatory, the Protestants also denied Hell. This is easily understood. Suppose we are burying Uncle Fred, who only went to Mass when the weather was fine, or when he was feeling like it, and you have to say a few words about his condition or state in the after-life. With only the two alternatives to choose from, how, on earth are you going to tell everybody, his grieving widow and his offspring, that Fred is in Hell? No, you will just be able to celebrate his life as they do nowadays. And Hell is done away with! As I believe I said at the beginning of this discourse on Purgatory, the majority of good teachers of Catholicism generally accept that most people go to Purgatory. I remember when I was working alongside Don José María Hernandez Garnica, (one of the first three priests of Opus Dei) and I happened to make some negative comment about the sorry state of the Church and society and said that a lot of people who go sliding into Hell. He interrupted with the remark that 90% of Catholics would go to Purgatory, because that was what the Church was about, to save souls.

Nevertheless, I have a sneaking suspicion that the numbers might have gone down since 1970. And what are we to do? Very simply follow the advice of the Second Book of Maccabees, where it says, '*it is a holy and a wholesome thing to pray for the dead that they may be released from their sins*' (2 Macc 12:46). This is the clinching argument in favour of Purgatory. The Reformers, as I might have mentioned, say it is an invalid argument, given that this book does not belong to the Canon, that is the list of approved books of the Old Testament. *Correction*, does not belong to the Canon of the books of the Old Testament, in the Protestant Bible, *as compiled by Martin Luther.*

Of course, there are other passages in the New Testament which we are all agreed upon. One, that draws our attention is Matthew 5: 26 where it tells you that having been cast into prison (Purgatory) you will not be let out until you have paid the last farthing (the present-day translation is a penny). This bit means that in God's justice, every single sin will have to be atoned for. St Padre Pio says amongst his writings something similarly striking, except that he says each one of our sins was paid for by each one of Our Lord's sufferings! What is the conclusion we must draw from these reflections?

Very simply, that we have to fight hard not to accumulate lots of faults and failings that we will have to pay for in Purgatory, assuming we get there. And on a more positive note, to pray intensely for the holy souls who are there.

Do you believe in ghosts? A lot of people, who don't want to be thought credulous or naive in any way, say they do not. But I am quite sure that they do exist. God, very kindly allows souls who are nearer the exit of purgatory, to hasten their release, by reminding us who remain here on earth, to pray for them. I remember, St Josemaría telling us once about a car journey in the early days of Opus Dei with a few of his sons in the Work, asking the driver to stop when they passed by a cemetery, and he asked them all to get out on the spot and say prayers for the dead. When they got back in the car, he apologised for causing a delay on their journey saying how when he was a young priest how they - the holy souls - tugged on his cassock to make him pray for them. What is also quite clear is that he used to say a special prayer for the holy souls every day after Holy Communion. Now I ask myself, do I pray regularly for those who have died, particularly for those I have known in life? And then we may be sure that they pray for us. One author I read once said they pray very intensely and their prayers are very effective despite the fact that they cannot pray for themselves.

HELL

WHAT I FEEL LIKE SAYING at the present moment about this topic is well let's get it over with! And I am sorry to say that is precisely what you cannot do. St Faustina on her way out of Hell as she describes in her Diary or Memoirs, tells us that one clear notion came to her mind, that was that the majority of people in Hell were the people who did not believe in it. Statistics lead us to believe that, unfortunately, in today's society, most people pour scorn on the notion. So, we have to ask why? The main reason is that the idea that we should go to Hell is too shocking; that we should be condemned to suffer for all eternity. It is, of course, one of the mysteries of religion: so we need faith to believe in its existence. And part of our apostolate consists in convincing people of its reality, or its existence, and then, that they could be condemned to going there. Here is the well-known point of *The Way*, no.749:

> 'There is a hell. A statement which to you, might seem unoriginal and trite. I'm going to repeat it for you: there is a hell! Echo it for me, at the right moment, in the ear of that companion of yours… and of that other one'.

In order to come to some understanding and acceptance of the mystery we have to tackle it in parts. This will follow on what, at least in my own experience, the particular difficulties people have. Some, in fact, seem to have the lot. No matter. First of all, because people do not like pain of any kind, any mention of pain or suffering they find repugnant, even though it is someone else's fate. Then there is the duration and the measurement of the sin against the duration one has to suffer. How can anyone be bad enough to suffer? Where is God's justice? Now that is a good question because at the bottom of the misunderstanding is precisely misunderstanding of justice and in particular, God's justice. In addition to that, we need to include in our arguments further reference to Hope and Love. Now, the question is: where to begin?

First of all, a brief mention has to be made about public rejection of the true nature of Hell by the Millenarists, or Kyliasts. They were people, quite early on in the history of the Church, who, because of their compassion towards the inmates of Hell, decided to reduce its duration to 1,000 years, hence the name. The most famous exponent was Origen. There is nothing very difficult to see in their error. It is based on the simple fact of good people's compassion. Now, the same thing might be said of people who are reading these pages; they too will probably feel sorry for the people in Hell. My first observation is based on one of my feeble attempts to address this problem indirectly in trying to help a group of young people who were travelling in the same train as myself a few years ago. It started with a chance remark of one of the boys in the group. He said his cousin had been diagnosed with cancer and told he only had about a year to live. When he had made this announcement, he added, 'if this had happened to me it wouldn't bother me, because, I would just have a rollicking good time before the end'. It was abundantly clear that he and the others in the group were fully convinced that when death came there was nothing after. At which I thought, I cannot let this pass. But what if you are not ready to face God?

At which, another, a girl this time said 'but there is nothing after'. And I said justice demands there must be some settling of accounts: how is it possible that someone like Adolf Hitler who bumped off six million Jews could do that and get away with it? At which the young lady retorted, 'how do you know that there were six million'?

Unfortunately, we had just pulled into Huddersfield Station and they all got out, leaving me frustrated and unable to clinch the argument. After all, the numbers whether right or wrong matter but don't really matter, because the point is the question of justice. Hitler, and many like him, have been grossly unjust, and those whom he killed deserve retribution. In life, which is the time of mercy, we are granted forgiveness by God and indeed the opportunity to make amends. But, as we have seen, when death overtakes us, this opportunity is lost. In Dante's *magnum opus: 'The Divine Comedy'*, inscribed over the door of Hell, he has written: *'Abandon hope all ye who enter here'*.

The reason is that the people in Hell have no hope of reaching Heaven, they are confined to Hell for all eternity. At this point, people who feel compassion for the poor souls in Hell are saying how can it be possible for people to be condemned to endless pain for just one sin? The answer to this conundrum is given by St Thomas who says: *'The eternity of pain does not correspond to the <u>gravity</u> of the guilt, but corresponds to the <u>irreparable nature</u> of the guilt'*.

In other words, the soul goes to Hell, goes because it is not in a state of grace, as I mentioned before, quoting Frank Sheed, and so no longer has the power to live in Heaven. They are there because of the state they are in, the state of sin, which has eliminated grace. They are clinging on to the sin instead of confessing it and recovering the state of grace, so you will find, in addition, their soul is opposed to God, and we might say with hatred of God. In Medjugorje on 10th January 1983, Mirjana told Fr Tomislav Vlasic the following: 'I asked her (the Gospa - Our Lady) why God was so merciless in sending sinners to Hell for eternity'. She said:

> *'Men who go to Hell no longer want to receive any benefit from God. They do not repent nor do they cease to swear and to blaspheme. They make up their mind to live in Hell and do not at all contemplate leaving'. (This choice is irreversible).'* Quoted from the Marian Spring Centre, Surrey.

Of course, we do not have to believe these messages. However, what is expressed fits in with the rational explanation that if we have been destined for God and instead of corresponding, we rebel, what can we expect? It would be like driving our Jaguar car at full tilt at a tungsten steel wall. The faster we go, the harder the ensuing destruction. While on earth, our will is completely free, until the very last minute. God's mercy is open as long as life lasts, but when death overtakes us, the will is fixed, so-to-speak, in its attitude of love or hatred towards Almighty God.

Referring to our end, to be united with God. Obviously, it is in our nature to be satisfied with nothing less than union with God. And so, when it does not happen the soul is totally frustrated: this is given the name of the pain of loss. It has to be said, however, in both St Teresa's account of Hell, in the story of her Life, (Chapter 32), and in St Faustina's Diary, that more disagreeable things occur in Hell. In the Parable of the wedding feast, where a man is found to be without the wedding-garment, he is cast into <u>outer darkness</u>, and thus one of the afflictions is not being able to see anything except the tormenting devils. This is the company the inmates of Hell endure. In the play Man and Superman by George Bernard Shaw, he has one of the characters saying in a joking manner, 'I would rather go to Hell, rather than Heaven', 'and why'? asks his companion. 'Because the people there would be more interesting'.

Unfortunately, Shaw could not have thought it through, he was forgetting that the inhabitants in Hell, while on earth could indeed have been beautiful and talented, but now in Hell, have lost the only true talent that counts: the power of loving. They are of course, full of self-love and have no time for anybody else. They are utterly and totally alone. *Vae soli (Woe to those who are alone)* In fact, they are incapable of communicating with any of the other inmates.

Finally, on a more personal note, which I have found useful in helping people to come to terms with the problem of being sympathetic towards those condemned to Hell. This, of course, is apart from listing those sins which seem the most evil of all, like murder, people consumed with envy and hatred of their fellowmen. We take our lead in this argument from a consideration of the Devil. First of all, the Devil is bent on tempting souls and leading them into Hell where he will torment them further. He is deliberately frustrating or trying to frustrate God's determination to win souls for Heaven. God is Love, and He has become man in order to live and die for the salvation of souls. His love is a burning love and He longs for as many souls as possible to enter into union with Him. But He leaves them with complete freedom to choose Him and so they are exposed to the three enemies: the world, the flesh and the Devil. We, on this earth, are tested to see whether we will choose God or not. During our life we frequently fall into sin, but God provides us with many graces to both avoid it and then to reject it through penance and Confession. But the Devil puts it into the hearts of some worse than others to lead others into sin. In my opinion, it is these persons who are most deserving of the punishment of Hell. I don't know if you have seen any of the 'Godfather' films. In one of them, one of the Mafia offers some money to another assassin to kill his enemy: there are two prices: (if I remember correctly) $10,000 for a straightforward murder, but an offer of $20,000 if you arrange for the victim to commit fornication and then kill him, thereby not just taking away his physical life but the death of his soul, by sending him to Hell. Clearly, this concept is diabolical, and much more understandable that there should be a place for someone so cruel as to want to send someone else to Hell. In other words, there are human beings who act diabolically and are just as deserving of Hell as the Devil himself! We don't know God well enough to realise how strong is His love and desire that all souls should be saved. He has died to achieve it, but then the Devil comes along to frustrate God's love: His Precious Blood is wasted. It is this love of God, this longing for the salvation of souls, and that they should avail themselves of Our Lord's Sacrifice that is the cause of Our Lady's great sorrow at the foot of the Cross.

The Mafia or the Mafiosi are not the only ones who scandalise others and lead them into sin, although perhaps not so clinically or cruelly. Our Lady of Fatima spoke to the little children, who did not really understand, that later on certain fashions would be introduced which would be displeasing to Jesus. She was referring, of course, to the way some women today, dress immodestly. I happened to read one of the communications of Medjugorje recently and Our Lady said some girls were going to Hell through vanity. At first, I wondered how this could be. Then I realised, from the words of the Gospel which talks about *'little ones who believe in me'* being scandalised. And, further, *'it is impossible that scandals should not come but woe betide the one who causes them' (Luke 17:1)*. But these girls do not realise that they are causing others to sin. I feel sure that this is the case with the majority but also there is no doubt that there are more sophisticated women who do know exactly what they are doing and set out to provoke interest and even incite others to sin. Perhaps when we examine our own conscience, we too may find there have occasions in which we have led other people into sin: casual words, caustic words, critical words, salacious words, careless words. The mind boggles! It is, unfortunately, very easy to be the cause of others' sins. Sometimes it is just cowardice, lack of courage, especially when we should reprove a fault in someone who depends on our judgement and for whom we are responsible. We have all been endowed with power of some kind, and if you are a priest, like me, an even greater responsibility. Many priests today, I am afraid, are reluctant to reprove faults and even sins.

Finally, a further explanation of Hell, which, of course, we would understand better if we understood God better. As we know, God cannot change, *apud Deum non est mutatio nec vicissitudinis obumbratio* St James tells us in his epistle. This means that if God makes a decision, that's it, he cannot go back on his word. Now we know that God loves all his creatures, both Angels and men. This burning love for each one has to continue, even when we sin, and even when we are confirmed in sin, when the soul is filled with hatred towards God. This then means that when souls are turned away from God, into the outer darkness of Hell, they will continue to rebel against God and are frustrated by Him, especially when He continues to love them. They have lost the power to love; they cannot love any more. The more He loves them the more they suffer. It is precisely because we are destined to unite ourselves with God, in Heaven, that this isolation from God in Hell is so painful. So now it is time to look into Heaven.

HEAVEN

IN MANY WAYS THIS IS a more difficult mystery. By this time, we will have discovered that all the mysteries of our Faith vary from one to another. Generally speaking, it is through the understanding of God that we understand all the other mysteries. This, obviously, is true of the understanding of Heaven, since Heaven means in essence the union of the soul with Almighty God, so really, if we understood God fully and properly, we should understand Heaven. If we die in a state of grace, this grace is transformed into what is called the Beatific Vision, the soul is then empowered with a special gift to enable it to see God. St John gives a glimmer of hope of understanding:

> 'Beloved, we are sons of God even now, and what we shall be hereafter, has not been made known as yet. But we know that when he comes, we shall be like him; we shall see him, then, as he is' (1 Jn 3:2).

This is telling us, indirectly, that it is through the likeness in our own soul that we have the capacity to see God. There is a saying in philosophy: *'cognoscit sibi simile'*; *('like knows like')*. During our lifetime we have to try to become more and more like Our Lord Jesus Christ. When this is brought to perfection, which is through the Beatific Vision, we see God, as in a new *species* or mirror which is our own soul. This explains why we have to spend our life on earth becoming more and more identified with Christ. And, in addition, ensuring our soul is pure and clean.

The trouble is that God always exceeds our capacity through His infinite splendour. That is why we have attached a rider in the form of St Paul's saying (which of course was taken from the Prophet Isaiah):

> *'The eye has not seen, nor ear heard, neither has it entered into the heart of man to conceive the things that God has prepared for those who love him' (1 Cor 2:9).*

This is telling us the obvious: that we cannot imagine the infinite splendour and majesty of God. It brings us down to earth, so-to-speak. We are clearly not in the same league as God. He so transcends the world, and all his creatures. Although there is a certain community of nature, there is, strictly speaking, no comparison. So, these reflections are basically negative. We have, in other words, to be patient. One day we shall see God, but while we are here on earth, we have to content ourselves with the hope of Heaven, reflecting on Our Lord's encouraging words: *'Fear not, little flock for your Father has promised you a kingdom' (Lk 12:32).*

Thus, it is clear we must never lose hope of one day attaining that happiness which God alone can give. Meanwhile, we must also realise the folly of attempting to make heaven out of earth. Heaven is Heaven, union with God. St Paul tells us *'Quae sursum sunt quaerite' ('Seek the things that are above') (Col 3:1).* Many people keep their eyes cast down, wallow in the base satisfactions of this world. They are materialistic they think that satisfying their senses is the ultimate satisfaction, despite the fact that God continually tells us we must seek Him and the Heaven He has promised us. This means we must foster the virtue of Hope, the virtue by which we hold on to Heaven.

At this point I think it is appropriate to quote what St Thomas Aquinas tells us in his commentary on the *Credo*:

> *'It is fitting that reference should be made to the end of all our desires at the end of the Symbol when it says: 'Vitam aeternam, Amen''.*

In eternal life the most important thing is that a man is joined to God. For God is the reward and end of all our labours. *'Ego protector tuus sum, et merces tua magna nimis'* ('I am your protector and your exceedingly great reward'). This joining up with God consists in perfect vision. *'Videmus nunc per speculum in aenigmate; tunc autem facie ad faciem'* ('We see now darkly as in a mirror, then we shall see face to face') *(1Cor 13:12)*. Likewise, as the Prophet says, it consists in supreme praise: *'Gaudium et laetitia invenietur in ea, gratiarum actio et vox laudis'* ('Happiness and rejoicing are found there and thanksgiving and the voice of praise') *(Is 51:3)*.

Likewise, in the perfect satisfaction of desire, for the blessed will have more than they can desire or hope for. The reason for this is that no-one can fulfil his desire in this life, nor can any created thing ever satisfy man's desire: God alone can satisfy him and infinitely exceeds his desire and hence it is that he cannot attain peace except in God, as Augustine says in his *Confessions*: *'Fecisti nos, Domine ad te, et inquietum est cor nostrum donec requiescat in te'* ('You have made us for yourself, Lord, and our heart will not rest until it rests in You').

And because the saints will have God perfectly in the homeland, it is clear that their desire will be satisfied and in glory will exceed it still more. And therefore, the Lord says: *'Totum gaudium non intrabit in gaudentes, sed toti gaudentes intrabunt in gaudium. Satiabor cum apparuerit gloria tua, et iterum: Qui replet in bonis desiderium tuum. Quidquid enim delectabile est, totum est ibi superabundanter. Si enim appetuntur delectationes'*. If delights are desired, there will be supreme and most perfect delight, because they are from the supreme good, namely God: *'Delectationes in dextera tua usque in finem'*.

'Likewise, it consists in joyful society of all the blessed; this society will be supremely delightful, because anyone will have all goods with all the blessed. For anyone will love another as himself, and therefore will rejoice in the good of another as if it were his own. In such a way that the happiness and joy of one will increase inasmuch as the joy of all'.

This last point is worth commenting on if only because of the contrast with our ways and attitudes on earth. How often, when we see another person's success or qualities we are filled with envy; and if this is with regard to spiritual virtues or grace, is in fact a sin against the Holy Spirit, whereas in Heaven we rejoice at another's success and happiness, as if it were our own. St Josemaría once passed a kind of casual remark concerning the attitude of St Joseph, as if witnessing the arrival in Heaven of our Blessed Lady, so beautiful and glorious, and when people in Heaven (presumably the Angels), asked: '*Who is She*'? (echoing the words of *The Holy Rosary*, a little book of reflections on the Mysteries of the Rosary written by St Josemaría.), St Joseph replied: '*My Wife*'!

Furthermore, as a kind of corollary of this, every time someone enters Heaven, we would feel a glow and happiness in sympathy with the sensation of happiness which was ours on entering eternal happiness.

As I think I mentioned in relation to the attitude of selfishness of the souls in Hell, by way of contrast, the souls in Heaven communicate freely all their joy and happiness as they gaily sing the praises of God. Some people, perhaps with a similar attitude to that of George Bernard Shaw, saying, how boring to sing the praises of God for all eternity and really consumed with self-love, resenting the glory attributed to the Blessed Trinity, and at bottom really wishing it were themselves who were being adored and loved. Or maybe it is simply that they are tone-deaf and cannot appreciate the beautiful melody of the Canticle and Song of the Angels.

THE INCARNATION

AT THIS STAGE IN THE proceedings we change tack. Instead of focusing our attention on ourselves, how we were created, and for what purpose, our deviations and sins, and the consequence of sin and the last things. We turn now to the remedy provided for us by Our Lord and Saviour Jesus Christ. Sometimes, while giving a retreat, I have been disappointed on finding people have arrived a day or two late, and missed the first part. Disappointed because I shared with Fr Michael Richards the idea that the first, rather negative part, was really the most important. You may disagree, and the very good reason for that opinion is here because now we are going to contemplate the figure of our Adorable Saviour, Christ Our Lord! And you can't do better than that. In 'Redemptor Hominis', n.13, John Paul says: '*as the Council teaches: 'by his Incarnation, he, the Son of God, in a certain way <u>united Himself with each man</u>'. This was taken from Gaudium et Spes, n. 22 'The Church therefore, sees its fundamental task as enabling that union to be brought about and renewed continually. The Church wishes to serve this simple end: that each person may be able to find Christ, in order that Christ may walk with each person the path of life, with the power of the truth about man and the world that is contained in the mystery of the Incarnation and the Redemption and with the power of love that is radiated by that truth.'*

THE HOLY HUMANITY OF JESUS CHRIST

Here is a quotation from *'Christ is Passing By'* (a book of homilies written by St Josemaría), which seems as if it were prompted by the Pope's words we have just quoted, although they were written much earlier. It is another case of 'great minds think alike': *'Every Christian should make Christ present among men. He ought to act in such a way that those who know him sense the 'fragrance of Christ'. Men should be able to recognise the Master in the disciples.'*

Then he goes on to say in another homily on Christ the King: *'You all experience a great joy in your souls as you consider the sacred humanity of Our Lord. He is a king with a heart of flesh, like yours; he is the author of the universe and of every creature, but he does not lord it over us. He begs us to give him a little love, as he silently shows us his wounds.*

Why then do so many people not know him? Why do we still hear that cruel protest: 'We do not want this man to reign over us? There are millions of people in the world who reject Jesus Christ in this way; or rather they reject his shadow, for they do not know Christ. They have not seen the beauty of his face; they do not realise how wonderful his teaching is. This sad state of affairs makes me want to atone to Our Lord. When I hear that endless clamour - expressed more in ignoble actions than in words - I feel the need to cry out, 'He must reign!'

OUR OWN UNION WITH CHRIST

Whenever we are challenged, even with the words of St Josemaría quoted above, which are quite a gentle remonstration, we tend to bristle, as if we are accused of being to blame for this ignorance in the world. Nobody is saying that you, personally are to blame. But we can do something about it, and, in the course of acquiring the knowledge of Christ's teaching and giving others an authentic picture of Jesus Christ, we shall also discover how we are perfected and uplifted in the process.

St John says in his Gospel *'This is eternal life, to know the one true God and Jesus Christ whom He has sent'*. And further, *'But no-one knows the Father except the Son and those to whom He has revealed Him'* (Jn 17:3).

Clearly, we should all like to know God, but we also know that because God is a Spirit, we cannot know Him directly. St Philip the Apostle asked Jesus in the Last Supper: *'Lord, let us see the Father; that is all we ask.'* And Our Lord replied: *'What, Philip, here am I, who have been all this while in your company; hast thou not learned to recognise me yet? Whoever has seen me, has seen the Father....'* (John 14: 8-9). Here is one of the great blessings of the Incarnation: it makes it possible for us to see God. However, we realise that we are still not able to see God directly. Moses, if you remember, in the Old Testament, wanted to see God. He is asked the same question and what does God say? It is all recorded in the book of Exodus.

> *'Give me, then, said Moses, the sight of thy glory. And He answered, All my splendour shall pass before thy eyes, and I will pronounce, in thy presence, my own divine name, the name of the Lord who shews favour where he will. But, my face, he said, thou canst not see; mortal man cannot see me, live to tell of it. Then, he said, there is a place here, close by me, where thou mayst stand on a rock; there I will station thee in a cleft of the rock, while my glory passes by, and cover thee with my right hand until I have gone past. So, when I take my hand away, thou shalt follow me with thy eyes, but my face thou canst not see'* (Ex 33:17).

So, there you have it, but expressed in a different way, nobody, that is, no ordinary human being can see God and still live. Regarding this, St Thomas says God is invisible but not in our usual way of saying something is invisible because it is too dark, as happens at night, with not enough light, but the opposite. No, God is too bright. He dazzles us.

A way of explaining this is by saying you cannot see the sun, because it is too bright. If you look at it directly it will blind you. The love of God is too much for us, in our ordinary condition on this earth, with our human eyes. In the Letter to the Hebrews we have a pithy statement: *'Deus noster ignis consumens est'* (*'God is a consuming fire'*) (Heb. 12:27). He is not just a fire, but a consuming fire. This is another example of what was mentioned earlier that His ways are not our ways. But fear not, God has it all worked out about He makes it possible for us to know Him and to see Him.

What do you do when the sun is shining too brightly? We don't usually come across this problem in England and especially where I live, in Manchester. Abroad, it is common. You avoid the sunny side of the street; you seek the shade. And, again, the Holy Spirit puts it into words for us in the Canticle of Canticles: *'Sub umbra illius quem desideraveram sedi'* (*'I sat down under the shadow of my well-beloved'*) *(Cant. 2:3)*. And who is my well-beloved? Why Jesus of course! The sacred humanity of Jesus Christ is my shade. Just as Jonah the Prophet who ran away and got swallowed up by a whale, found shade under a juniper tree which God made grow just for his benefit. So, we too, find cool refreshment in the shade or shadow from the bright light of God. St Paul says to Timothy: *'Lucem inhabitat inaccessibilem'* (*'God dwells in inaccessible light'*) *(I Tim 6:16)*. This is of course the eternal light of the Blessed Trinity, which, with the grace of God, one day we will contemplate by means of the Beatific Vision. Meanwhile here on earth, with the eternal light being too bright for us: *'Candor est lucis aeternae'* (*'The dazzling white of the eternal light'*) *(Wis 7:26)*, we have to get to know and love the most Holy Humanity of Christ, and seek the comfort and shade of His gentle arms.

Now to do this we need faith. We must fall in love with the most Holy Humanity of Jesus Christ. But if we see Him as merely a man, albeit the most wonderful specimen of the human race, we will, inevitably remain on a purely human level and fail in our purpose which is to be united to the Blessed Trinity. Nowadays, unfortunately, there are quite a lot of men who pass for theologians who do not accept that Jesus Christ is God. And still more unfortunately there are many more have been led astray by these so-called theologians who have resurrected the Arian heresy. *

* Arius was a monk from Alexandria who died 336 AD and said it was not the Second Person of the Trinity who became man, but the *logos* God's greatest creature, nevertheless, a creature that could grow and develop. He was condemned at Nicea 325.

One of the false notions spread around by these people is that they will use expressions that Christ is a human being and susceptible of change. We know it says in the Gospel of St Luke that Jesus *'advanced* in wisdom with the years...' (Luke 2:52) but this applies only to His human nature which acquired experimental knowledge of the world like other men, but not to his Divine nature endowed with God's knowledge and wisdom.

Well, after this digression, we bring to mind the insistence of St Josemaría, especially at the beginning of Opus Dei on having a living, operative faith. This is beautifully expressed in *The Way* no. 584:

> 'Stir up the fire of your faith. - Christ is not a figure who has passed. He is not a memory that is lost in history. He lives!: Jesus Christus heri et hodie: ipse et in saecula! St Paul: Jesus Christ yesterday and today and forever!'

And why this insistence? For one thing it brings to mind that all these actions of Jesus Christ are God's actions; we are learning about God. For another that the human nature is like a vehicle transporting God's love and goodness to us. It brings us the light and happiness of God's life into our life. When Jesus Christ spoke on the mountain, depending on the acoustics, He was heard by hundreds of individuals. But since His words which are divine, transcend the circumstances and individuals to whom they were immediately directed, they apply to us in the twenty-first century today and they are spoken to millions throughout the centuries. An example may help. When Jesus was praying in the Garden of Olives, plunged in grief and sadness over the world's sins, and turns to his Apostles for company and consolation, saying: *'Could you not watch an hour with Me?' (Mt 26:40)*, he was saying it to me too as I dozed off in my meditation. When Martha goes back to her sister Mary who had stayed on in the house, when Jesus arrived at Bethany, and says to her: *'Magister adest et vocat te'* (*'The Master is here and is calling you'*) *(John 11:29)*. It means that Jesus is calling us also. The trouble is that we don't exercise our faith as we should. We should apply it all the time when we read the Scriptures. What is God saying to me here? I must ask myself: What is He trying to tell me? What is his message? And since it is the Gospel, the Good News, it will always be elevating, enlightening and exciting. If we have faith.

IMITATION OF CHRIST

As a summary of what has just been said, the upshot of it all should be that we end up being like Jesus Christ. St Josemaría in several passages of his writings encourages us to read and re-read the words of the Gospel, so that they are imprinted indelibly on our memory and we see Him, as he puts it, as if in a film or moving-picture.

In this way, even if we haven't got a New Testament to hand, we can recapture the scenes in our imagination. First of all, though, we have to make sure we don't do any diagonal reading, that is, reading as though we shall get a prize for finishing first. No, we should drink the Gospel in, as chickens drink, not as horses. When I was little, Lipton's Tea Van came down the back street pulled by a horse. When it drank from the horse-trough it put its mouth down and sucked up the water at an enormous speed. Because of its big nostrils, it could breathe at the same time as drink. What a contrast with the way that chickens drink, in such a refined lady-like manner. They, in common with other birds have no swallowing mechanism, they lower their beak into the water, take in a few drops, lift their head aloft, look from right to left, and repeat the process. Well, that is how we should drink in the teaching of the Sacred Scripture; dipping into it, abstracting a few words, a phrase, then raising our heads to Heaven, and meditate a while to absorb what we have taken in. And what will we find?

We will find, if we don't put any obstacles in the way that imperceptibly we become more supernatural. The principles and purposes of the Gospels will gradually overtake our excessively human outlook; in short, we will become more Christ-like. Nevertheless, I see no harm in suggesting we might pick up some of Our Lord's more commonly occurring characteristics. I have to concede that this insight belongs to St Josemaría. In particular, one of the points in *The Way*, no. 829: '*Didn't you see Jesus' eyes light up when the widow left her little alms in the temple?...*' This reveals that St Josemaría has spotted something about Our Lord that is not immediately evident: his appreciation of generosity. But this also applies to lots of other virtues manifested by individuals in the Gospel. He really values faith, as we see in His comments about the Roman Centurion and the Syrophoenician woman. He is obviously impressed on seeing little Zacchaeus's enterprise in climbing the tree so as to see Jesus. As a matter of fact, it is easier for us. Zacchaeus was not aware of what Our Lord had achieved in becoming Man, and much less of what He would be going through in about a year's time, in order to be walking along the road towards his home. We, on the other hand, can see more easily what He has done for us and make our efforts in gratitude. With a number of virtues, Our Lord specifically records his appreciation of them or deliberately recommends them as when He lists the Beatitudes, or tells people to obey the Holy Will of God, learn from Him to be humble and meek of heart, or to pray without ceasing.

Clearly, there is a fundamental need to approach the Gospels in a spirit of humility and docility. I have found, myself, how helpful it is to copy St Josemaría in repeating his act of adoration and faith, on beginning to pray, saying: *My Lord and my God, I firmly believe that you are here, that you see me, that you hear me. I ask you for pardon of my sins, and grace to make this time of prayer fruitful.* When in Rome, over fifty years ago, attending several of St Josemaría's meditations, on two occasions, he paused over the words – 'firmly believe' - and turned round towards us to declare **'it is an act of faith'**. At the time, it certainly helped to put me in the presence of God and profit from the period of mental prayer we were just starting. From then onwards we can start our dialogue with Jesus. Nothing more is required, except of course a generous response to his promptings. *'Exaudiam quid loquatur in me Dominus'* ('I will hear what the Lord God will speak in me') (Ps. 84, 9). But are we ready to take notice of what Our Lord God will want? Very often we don't hear because His demands are too heavy, or, so we suppose. But we should realise that when God makes demands on us, He also gives us His grace to help us to carry them out.

IMMANUEL

The name given by the prophet, Isaiah, to the son who would be born of Mary, our Mother, was Immanuel, which means God is with us. However, God wants more than just to be with us, He wants to live in us. When we receive Holy Communion, we are well aware that this is the fulfilment of the Psalm - the Lord is my Shepherd - who leads me to green pastures, in other words, he feeds me. He is my crook and my staff, that is to say He supports me. But what does God Himself get out of this? The answer is very simple. He gets to live in us, which then enables Him to live on earth once more, through us. This is what St Peter Eymard tells us:

> 'Holy Communion not only gives to the sacramental Jesus the opportunity to satisfy His love; it gives Him a new life which He will consecrate to the glory of His Father.... Something divine will then come to pass in the one who communicates; man will labour, and Jesus will give the grace of labour; man will keep the merit, but to Jesus will be the glory; Jesus will be able to say to His Father: 'I love Thee, I adore Thee, and I still suffer, living anew in My members! This what gives Communion its highest power; it is a second and perpetual incarnation of Jesus Christ; between Jesus Christ and man it forms a union of life and love; in a word, it is a second life for Jesus Christ.'

I have often thought that these words of St Peter Eymard are a kind of explanation of the well-known prayer 'O Iesu vivens in Maria', which goes on to say: 'veni et vive in famulis tuis, in spiritu sanctitatis tuae, in plenitudine virtutis tuae, in perfectione viarum tuarum, in veritate virtutum tuarum, in communione mysteriorum tuorum; dominare omni adversae potestate, in spiritu tuo ad gloriam Patris. Amen'. Which, when translated loosely reads: 'Oh Jesus, living in Mary, come and live in your servants, in a spirit of holiness, in the fullness of your power, in the perfection of your ways, in the truth of your virtues, in the communion of your mysteries and dominate over every adverse power, in your spirit for the glory of the Father Amen'.

From this it is clear that not only is the soul in the closest possible union with Christ, but also qualifies as an Apostle who is able to reproduce with his life the virtues and goodness and the love of Our Lord Jesus Christ. And so, with Jesus living within us in this way, living His life all over again in us, we become *alter Christus,* another

Christ, or as St Josemaría used to say, more than that, *ipse Christus, Christ Himself*. Just imagine, if all Christians were like that, other Christs! It would mean that the whole world would be renewed and given back to God; everybody would be able to come back to God. Christ would truly reign!

THE MYSTERY OF THE INCARNATION

According to St Thomas, God is *Ipsum Esse Subsistens*. He is pure Being. He has no essence in the way we have. We are composite beings. In man as in everything in the predicamental order; there is a composition of essence and the act of being. In God there is no composition: He just *is*, He is *esse*. *Each* of the three Persons in God, that is to say, the Father, the Son and the Holy Spirit, has this *esse*. Father *is*, the Son *is*, the Holy Spirit *is*. And they are by virtue of the *esse*, that is to say, the act of being by which they are. Now, of the three, it is the Second Person whom we call the Son, who became incarnate through the Blessed Virgin Mary. So it is through the *esse* carried by the Second Person, that Jesus Christ Our Lord, <u>is</u>. His being or *esse*, which He has in common with the other two divine Persons is divine. The Person of the Son is, so-to-speak, the vehicle which provides the being of Christ, which is divine. The divine Person is united to the human nature taken from the virginal womb of the Blessed Virgin Mary, and makes this human nature *to be*. This means that the human nature <u>is</u> by means of the *actus essendi given* to it by the Person. Theologians will say that the Union between the Divine Nature and the human nature is Hypostatic, that is, via the Divine Person. So, in order to love Jesus Christ, it is important to know Him, at least to the extent we are able and He is God. Not taking note of this, addressing Him as if He were a human being like me, is to insult Him. An example should suffice. In Our Lord's Passion, He was gravely insulted and blasphemed. A soul truly in love with Jesus is correspondingly saddened on seeing Jesus treated in this way. That is why it is so helpful to ask Our Lady to accompany us in our meditation on Our Lord's sufferings. Hey! This is my Lord you are insulting! What are you about?

So, we see how clarifying the doctrine and being precise makes a great deal of difference to our attitude and ultimately to our love and tenderness towards God.

From what has been said about the Incarnation we realise several things that, in meditating on Our Lord's life, which we will do shortly, we need certain virtues. We have mentioned faith and love, but we also need to think about humility. In this aspect we learn a lot from Our Lady. There is a wonderful passage in *'Friends of God'* which brings to the fore how Our Lady's mind worked. We don't often think about it but it has to be taken into account that because Our Lady was conceived immaculate, that is to say, she was not affected by Original Sin, her mind was absolutely clear and she had wonderful perception. We, on the other hand, are stupid in comparison. It is, I am sure, because of this that St Josemaría had this beautiful **insight** recorded in the homily on Humility in *'Friends of God'* as follows:

> *'Mary becomes transformed in holiness in the depths of her most pure heart on seeing the humility of God: 'the Holy Spirit shall come upon you, and the power of the Most High shall overshadow you; and therefore the Holy One to be born of you shall be called the Son of God'. The Blessed Virgin's humility is a consequence of that unfathomable depth of grace which comes into operation with the Incarnation of the Second Person of the Blessed Trinity in the womb of his ever-Immaculate Mother'.*

We have here a wonderful example of how Our Lady's mind works and it is showing us the way we, too, have to meditate. She perceives in God's action, the profound humility of God in lowering Himself to take on our human nature and become Man.

Was it this that inspired St Paul to write those beautiful words in the second chapter of his Epistle to the Philippians: *'exinanivit semetipsum formam servi accipiens'* (*'emptied himself taking the form of a slave …'*) *(Phil 2:7).* Or maybe it inspired the writer of the Hymn, Te Deum to declare halfway through, *'non horruisti virginis uterum'* (*'you did not abhor the virgin's womb'*). What right have we be to be proud on reflecting on God's own humility? Why should we not follow his invitation to learn from him to be meek and humble of heart?

I have taken up quite a lot of space to reflect on the Incarnation, but I think you must agree that such a mystery deserves to be given a lot of attention. No sooner has Our Lady given her assent: *'Ecce ancilla Domini, fiat mihi secundum verbum tuum'* (*'Behold the handmaid of the Lord, let it be done to me according to thy word'*) *(Lk 1:38)*, than she sets off with haste into the hill-country to visit her cousin Elizabeth. St Josemaría liked the expression: *cum festinatione - with haste*. It is rich in significance. It expresses with the minimum of words the love which fills Our Lady's heart, and how she is anxious to serve her cousin in her need, very well aware that at her great age she will appreciate what Our Lady, with her youthful energy could provide, despite the fact that she herself was in the same condition, as an expectant mother. We can also draw another very important conclusion; that our Mother, Mary, watching over us, will exercise the same sentiments in our regard and come to our assistance in our life's troubles and temptations. The next thing, however, we should be looking at is what happened when Our Lady returned home, and what St Joseph was to think on seeing her unexpected condition.

THE BIRTH OF OUR LORD

I MAY HAVE MENTIONED THIS before, but there is no harm in mentioning it again given its importance. It is the saying of St Thomas Aquinas: *'Actio Christi fuit nostra instructio'* (*'the actions of Christ were for our instruction'*).

That is to say, whatever Our Lord did during his time on earth was to teach us a lesson. As he himself said *'I am the Way, the Truth and the Life'* (*Jn 14:6*). He is showing us the way to behave. If we are ever in any doubt as to what to do, what action to take, we open the pages of the Holy Gospel and we have the answer. This also applies to when Our Lord does not take any action at all. Even that is for our guidance. As a matter of fact, this applies very specially when Our Lord is born. His acceptance, as a little child, of being born, being washed and clothed, being fed, being embraced by Mary and Joseph are of paramount importance. What human beings find very hard to accept is that being small or of being of little significance, or simply, taking no action is a thing most pleasing to God. In the Old Testament, we find the saying *'My delights are to be with the children of men, playing with them in the world'* (*'ludens in orbe terrarum'*) (*Prov 8:31*). We are God's children: I hate to say this, but we are like toys. He is often playing with us as children play with their toys. From time to time, he picks us up, and puts us down, seems to pay us a lot of attention, but then leaves us alone. I have learnt this from reading St Therese of Lisieux, and also from St Josemaría Escriva, who once put it like this: **'I have seen wonderful things in my life, my son, but then he leaves you alone, you know, and you have to remain faithful'**. (This was said during a telephone conversation with a member of Opus Dei called Jaime Sanchez). It is, of course, God's way of acting for our good, which he always has at heart. At the time, it may be a mystery to us but it always has a meaning. When joys come, we are of course, delighted, but when it is sorrow instead, we feel the pain. I believe it is on record, in *Christ is Passing By*, that St Josemaría said, '*when God sends us pleasant things in life, that is God saying: that is how much I love you. And when he sends us unpleasant things, that is God asking: and how much do you love me*'?

Well, how does this apply to the Birth of Jesus Christ? You might well say, 'not at all'. I am just so happy contemplating the scene. It is true that Jesus Christ Our Lord, who has deigned to come down from Heaven to earth, has just been given a mighty insult by the human race in the form of the inhabitants of Bethlehem: '*He came unto his own and his own received him not*' *(Jn 1:11-13)*. But we are enthralled, filled with love and an extraordinary joy on seeing the love and tenderness with which our Mother Mary and our father and Lord, St Joseph treat Jesus. Joseph does everything in his power to find somewhere for him to be born, which is, in the end, a poor stable, meant for animals, and so Mary wraps Jesus tenderly in swaddling clothes and places him a manger. Blessed Alvaro once remarked: '*and why did Mary cover Our Lord in the swaddling clothes? It was to protect his tender skin from being hurt by the hard straw in the manger*'. She is saying to herself and naturally to her Saviour, 'how much I love you my Son, Oh how much I would love to surround you with the comfort and rich covering you deserve, but I will surround and cover you with my love instead'.

St Jerome says: '*Whenever I look at the spot where my Saviour was born, I begin a fond conversation with him. O my Jesus, I say, what a hard bed you have there in the manger, all for the sake of my salvation. How shall I ever repay you for it?*

Then it seems to me as if the Babe answers: I ask nothing but that you sing, Glory to God on high!

Then I go on: But, Beloved mine, I must give you something. I will give you all my money.

But he replies: All Heaven is mine and the earth. I have need of nothing. Give it to the poor, and I will take it as given to me.

I continue: Gladly will I do that. But I just must give you something too, or I shall die of grief. And the Babe answers: If you are so generous, then I will tell you what you shall give me. Give me your sins, give me your bad conscience and your damnation.

I say: What do you mean to do with that?

And the Babe says: I want to take it upon my shoulders, for that is my glory and my boast that I would take upon myself your sins and do away with them.

Then, old man that I am, I burst into tears and say: O little Child, dear little Child! How you have touched my heart! Take what is mine, give me what is yours. Then I shall be rid of my sins and sure of eternal salvation.'

When I read St Jerome's prayer for the first time, and remembering what I had learnt previously about him; how austere he was, living a lonely life, a man who was as hard as nails and so on, I must say I surprised to discover how tender-hearted he was. It shows how intimacy with Jesus softens the heart. This, in itself, is a way to grow in spiritual childhood, which in turn leads to humility.

The Second Person of the Blessed Trinity condescended to become man, taking our poor human nature and coming amongst us. What an extraordinary gesture! And we need to remember that when God decides to do something, that is for good and all, He can't go back on His word. The action is completely irreversible. And what did He expect of His creatures? He has come down from His throne in Heaven to save us from our sins. Ingratitude, as we know, is unknown in Heaven. Not so on earth, unfortunately, what do you think was the response from the children of men? Blank. Nothing. As if it had not happened. One has bought a farm, one a pair of oxen, one has married a wife, so they are totally taken up with their own concerns. They haven't got time for God; they are too busy with their own affairs. Many will say, *'Oh, but it was not spelt out for me'*. But even if there had been just a whisper that Almighty God had come down from Heaven and become man to sacrifice Himself for us don't you think this would have deserved further enquiry? Don't you think it deserves some investigation? It is, in a sense, too outrageous a gesture to be ignored. But no, people prefer to remain in blissful ignorance. Or is it fear of what God will say or do if He finds them not wearing a wedding garment! And unfortunately, in the end, this contrived ignorance is anything but blissful!

So, we see how, no sooner has Our Lord, come down from Heaven, to dwell amongst us, than he evokes feelings and emotions of love and tenderness. But God of course, is hoping for a bit more. He wants us to show our affection, but also to manifest our love in deeds. This is where the Shepherds and the Wise Men come in.

By their actions the shepherds demonstrate the attitude God wants to see in his creatures on earth. The inhabitants of Bethlehem did nothing for God made man, whilst the humble shepherds and the Kings kneel to adore him. Just the other day I heard a priest say, 'isn't it wonderful that when we expose the Blessed Sacrament, more people go to Confession'? (I believe I heard him say that Adoration and Confession seem to go together).

So, on going to be with Jesus, as we kneel and adore him, we are immediately inclined to seek his love and forgiveness. Jesus Christ our Saviour is born. The Angels announce the great news! '*Gloria in excelsis Deo, et in terra pax hominibus bonae voluntatis*'. ('*Glory to God in the highest and peace to men on earth of good will*') (*Lk 2:14*). Peace, the happiness of all the Angels and Saints in Heaven, with God, is what God Our Lord wants for all his people. If only they would have good will and love in their hearts! Unfortunately, they are so often swayed by the temptations of the world, the flesh and the Devil, to seek themselves instead. Can they not see how God himself seeks only the welfare of others, so forgetting himself, leaving the comfort and warmth of Heaven, He comes to bring us peace and happiness. He is clearly demonstrating the beauty of the virtue of poverty. If God deprives himself of the bare necessities of life, why are we so concerned about material things? If God clothes the lilies of the field so well, looks after the birds of the air and feeds them, why are we so anxious? We forget that our Father-God loves us much more than He loves irrational creatures. But not only do we worry about having food, clothing and shelter but we fight over it. The world, as we know, is in a sorry state. Many people are starving in different parts of the world. Why is this? The simple answer is because other people are too greedy. I have heard it said that in the Western World, comprising one third of the world's population, we eat two thirds of the world's food. This shows that it is a problem of unequal distribution, not that there is a real shortage. Then people come along and say we ought to limit the number of people on earth so there is enough food to go round. And guess what? These ones are in fact the greedy ones who create the shortage. They want to solve the problem by birth control instead of practising temperance and poverty. From this it is easy to see why this is the first lesson Jesus Christ teaches us as he appears on earth. For ourselves this is the opportunity for us to look at our own lives and see how well we live this virtue.

When St Francis of Assisi was commissioned by Jesus to restore his Church which was falling apart, this was the injunction he was given: to proclaim the holy Lady of Poverty. It was a way of telling the members of the Church to restrain their tendency to seek material prosperity. Unfortunately, the lesson seems to have been forgotten. Nevertheless, you and I should look at our own lives and examine our attitude towards material things; to see how we live detachment. St Josemaría had a number of questions which he suggested we should ask ourselves to see how we are living the virtue of poverty: *have I anything superfluous? Do I hoard any things I do not use? Do I look upon anything as my own, that is in my possession? When choosing do I pick what is least attractive?* More questions can be added to the list as we carry out our personal meditation.

THE HIDDEN LIFE

FROM THE TIME OUR LORD was born until he began his public life, He remains hidden and silent. Remember now the golden rule: the action of Christ is for our instruction; Jesus is showing us how to act, which from the very beginning is being hidden and silent. But was Christ inactive? Of course not. He was known later on in his public life as the carpenter. *'Isn't this the carpenter's son?..... And they had no confidence in him'* (*Mt 13:55*). That was because of their familiarity with him, or so they thought. But you and I know that they did not really know him, although they thought they did. Then again, Our Lord dressed like everybody else, and that was why, in the Garden of Gethsemane, Judas had to point Our Lord out by kissing him: because he was dressed like everybody else. And so, we ask why? The answer is, as always, because he wanted to set ordinary people, like you and me, an example. All through his hidden life, working, fetching and carrying water from the well, making a living in a humble occupation, shaping wood into useful furniture: doors, tables, chairs or whatever, he is telling us that any kind of occupation can be undertaken by us in the same way, and be a means of glorifying God, our Father. Of course, since Our Lord is God, he is always in the presence of God, and offering everything to his Father. We, on the other hand, have to make a definite, clear effort to remember God and that we are in his presence. We have to set our stall out, so-to-speak, and make an offering to God. We have to say to him, here, Lord, this is for you, and then we examine what we have done to see if it is really worthy of God. He is, after all, the Lord of the Universe, and we must make sure that what we have 'created' is up to the standard established by God in creation. This leads us on to think about St Josemaría and his love for little things. His emphasis on this makes us think straightaway about the Little Flower and how she too said this is how we show our love for God. St Josemaría and she have a lot in common but I would venture to say that St Josemaría took this method a step further. St Therese lived, by our standards, a very secluded existence, her experience and consequently her recommendations about what to offer God, were confined to that experience. The examples that come to my mind are; she tells us how she loved to tidy her sisters' cloaks in the cloakroom and put them on the peg; or that one day when one of the sisters inadvertently splashed her with dirty water while doing the laundry, she offered the unpleasant feeling to God as a small sacrifice. Everything she carried out with love, of course, and that was the basic recommendation. But St Josemaría has in mind all the many thousands of souls who are following his way, and they are in all kinds of professions in the world, and have to discover that the teaching about the value of little things can apply in every circumstance that occurs.

I remember hearing the author Andrew Vazquez de Prada, in a talk he once gave, saying that in his view, St Josemaría regarded material things as if they were sacred. When I was in Rome, sometimes St Josemaría would say, '*Come on, let's do Opus Dei*', and proceeded to go round the house straightening the furniture, closing a window properly. On another occasion, St Josemaría rang through to the sitting-room of the House of the Arches, part of Villa Tevere, to ask if some of the lads there could go round to the Villa, to hang up some curtains which were draped over the settees in the hallway, which the Staff had had to leave because they were too heavy for them, and the Father said, '***I am sorry to impose on you this way, but I want to spend the night thanking God for his goodness, for starting the Work, and all His blessings. But I can't do that with things out of their place. Things out of their place, do not give glory to God.***'

I wonder if we are like that; unable to pray because we have left our desk in a mess, or disorder in a drawer? I would wager we just leave things as they are, without caring to put things away. Although it may seem easy, looking after little things all the time and in all circumstances requires quite a lot of determination and will-power. It demands putting into practice the '*heroic minute*' quite often, overcoming laziness. We can help this along by remembering St Joseph in his workshop, or Our Lady washing clothes at the well. They would have kept the home at Nazareth spick and span, for Our Lord's sake, for God's glory.

OUR LORD'S HUMILITY

St Paul records a passage which some have denominated a hymn to humility in Chapter 2 of the Letter to the Philippians. It says: '*he humbled himself, taking the form of a servant, accepted an obedience, which led him to the Cross*' *(Phil 2:8)*. This was the pattern of Our Lord's whole life. Just imagine, the God who created the whole world, is now obeying Joseph and Mary, two of the creatures he has made. He was subject to them; St Luke says in his Gospel. '*Erat subditus illis*': '*he was subject to them*' *(Lk 2:51)*. This has got to make us think! How difficult it is, not just now and again, but always, to be obedient. We know that if we are to be saints, we have to stop, again and again, to ask the question, Lord, what do you want me to do now, and then, with the grace of God, to carry out what we see to be God's will, by being obedient to whoever is in authority. And very often this goes against our own inclination and preference. Nevertheless, this is the only way: and it was the way Our Blessed Lord chose. The thing is, of course, it that he need not have followed this way for his own sake, he did it to set us an example. In life, we have to be determined to follow the way of obedience in the same way Our Lord chose, as an example for others to follow. I remember Fr Dick Stork telling me that on one occasion, he heard an example given by Don Alvaro, now Blessed Alvaro, the Successor of St Josemaria. If I remember rightly, it took place in the house in Hampstead, London where St Josemaría and Blessed Alvaro were staying. While Dick was talking to St Josemaria, Blessed Alvaro approached with a letter he had been typing, and he showed it to him. St Josemaria took off his glasses and read the letter, and paused at some word or words, and said to Blessed Alvaro, '**this will need to be changed**', and without a word, of protest, or any explanation, he simply went away to make the correction. Obedience. It is not easy to fall in line, without registering our opinion. We always seem to have something to say or suggestion to make. Of course, when it is a big issue, no doubt the one with authority will add a rider to the effect that we are free to follow our preference. Even then, we should, interiorly, consult Our Lord's preference, casting our minds back to when St Gabriel made his proposal to Our Lady on God's behalf, and she said '*Quomodo fiet istud, quoniam virum non cognosco*'? ('*and how will this be done, since I know not man*'?) (Lk 1:34). She is asking for precision, in order to obey correctly. In a trice, the Archangel answers that it will be the Holy Spirit who will arrange things, and immediately she says '*Ecce ancilla Domini*' ('*I am the handmaid of the Lord, be it done unto me according to thy word!*') (Lk 1:38). As St Josemaría comments: '***how simply she said it. Another wonderful example for us to follow***'.

But Christ did not remain hidden and silent just to teach us the lesson of obedience. He was interested in remaining hidden for its own sake, we might say. Our Lord was, of course, in continual conversation with His Father and would be constantly talking to God the Father during his whole life. The trouble with us, is that very often we are not, so we find it hard to believe Jesus was continually in prayer.

OUR LORD'S LIFE OF WORK

Having said that, I may now seem to contradict it, by saying Jesus was also continually at work: '*My Father is at work, and I too must be at work (Jn 5:17)*. And what else was Jesus doing while working? He was praying also all the time and glorifying his heavenly Father. Since Jesus was God, is God, everything he did was supernatural. He sanctified his work all the time, everything he touched he supernaturalised and sanctified. We have to follow this example. In the book, '*Friends of God*', in the chapter entitled '*Working for God*', paragraph 56, St Josemaría writes:

> '*Our Lord's whole life fills me with love for him, but I have a special weakness for his thirty hidden years spent in Bethlehem, Gospels hardly mention, might seem empty of any special meaning to a person who views it superficially. And yet, I have always maintained that this silence about Our Lord's early life speaks eloquently for*

> *itself, and contains a wonderful lesson for us Christians. They were years of intense work and prayer, years during which Jesus led an ordinary life, a life like ours, we might say, which was both divine and human at the same time. In his simple workshop, unnoticed, he did everything to perfection, just as he was later to do before the multitudes'.*

So, this is what we, ordinary people, have to do, to get into Heaven. We have to imitate Jesus Christ, and sanctify our ordinary work each day. In all of this, following Jesus, we notice two things: one, that Our Lord did his work to perfection. It is inconceivable that his work should be slipshod, untidy. I think I already mentioned that anecdote about St Josemaría saying, on the eve of the 2nd October 1962, that he couldn't spend the night praying and thanking God for all his blessings, with things out of their place, - things out of place do not give glory to God! So, just imagine; could Jesus have pretended to offer his Father the offering of Cain, instead of the offering of Abel who gave God the best out of his flock of sheep? So, we have to do the best we can. And then, secondly, Our Lord sanctified everything he did. We should do the same, but we realise that while Our Lord did this as a matter of course, because being God he did everything supernaturally, we are just human. How can we make our offering supernatural? The answer is given by St Josemaría, of course. Whenever, he talked about work and making it supernatural he talked about the supernatural virtues, usually called the theological virtues, Faith, Hope and Charity. Like the three sisters who lived next door to my mother when she was young. In a Letter from Rome, dated 15 October 1948, we read:

> *'In our work, done face-to-face with God, - in his presence - let us pray without ceasing, for when we work as our spirit asks us to, we put into practice the theological virtues which crown Christian living. We practise faith, through our contemplative life, in this constant conversation with the Trinity present in our soul. We practise hope when we persevere in our work 'knowing that, in the Lord, you cannot be labouring in vain' (I Cor. 15: 58). We live*

> *charity, trying to put love of God into all our actions, spending ourselves in generous service of our brothers, men, of all souls.'*

I also call to mind, about thirty years ago, how Andrew Vazquez de Prada, having sent off his translation of the Dream of Gerontius, by St John Henry Newman, to St Josemaría, read out his reply to us in the get-together which, if my memory serves me right went more or less, as follows, *'May Jesus watch over you! Thank you, Andrew, for your book. Remember when you are at work always bear in mind the three theological virtues…I am glad to hear you have no problems, because that is how I like my sons to be'.* I hesitate to put any inverted commas because it is based on my recollection of what he read out from the letter. But what I am sure of is this expression about invoking the three virtues. As the years have gone by, I have found that St Josemaría never failed to mention them. The reason has to be the one I have intimated: Jesus Christ, as God, made all the material things he touched sacred. We cannot do the same; the best we can do is to exercise the supernatural virtues. Doing this they transform our work into something fitting for Almighty God. No doubt, Our Lady and St Joseph did the same, except of course, that they would work in close union with Our Lord.

OBEDIENCE

Another instance of the difference between Our Lord, and ourselves, especially where our activity is concerned, is that Jesus' mind and will worked in constant union with his heavenly Father. Instinctively, Our Lord, would do exactly what his Father would wish. He even went so far as to say this in answer to Our Lady's anguished question: *'My son why have you treated us so'? (Lk 2:48).* And he answered: *'did you not know that I must be about my Father's business' (Lk 2: 49),* as much as to say, I must always fulfil my Father's Will. Then, this makes sense out of the following words in St Luke's Gospel: *'He went down with them and was subject to them' (Lk 2:51).* We might say it is as if Jesus found his Father's will in his obedience to Mary and Joseph.

This has got to make us think. Here is God, who created the whole universe with a word, now in the human form of Jesus Christ, humbling himself, being completely at St Joseph's disposal. Ready to do just what Joseph asks of him, as his father. Here is a challenge indeed, for us wretched sinners, as we are, who through pride, with a mistaken idea of our own worth and dignity, puff ourselves up and resist the grace and opportunity of fulfilling God's will as presented by our parents or superiors. Of course, we find it hard to surrender our will. The freedom of our will is the most priceless gift from God that we possess. One almost could say that our life on earth consists in surrendering our will to God little by little until we can say with Our Lord as he died on the Cross, *'consummatum est'* (*'it is accomplished'*) (Jn 19:29), when we get to the end of our life on earth. Each time we come to the crossroads in life, we have to make a choice, and, with the grace of God, this will be the good choice, choosing to unite our will with God's will. Our Lady, as always, is the unique exception, for she always fulfilled God's holy will, from the age of three, if we accept St Brigid of Sweden's revelations. This would be very unusual for the ordinary person, but for Our Lady, not really so surprising, given that she was preserved by God from sin and its consequences, from the time of her conception. Bringing Our Lady into focus, ought to make us think how Our Lady's holiness is expressed. It coincides with that exclamation of a woman in the crowd *'blessed is the womb that bore thee'* and Our Lord's reply, *'Rather, blessed are they who hear the word of God and keep it'* (Lk 11:28). Our Lord is saying once more, that the most important characteristic of any human being is to be obedient. To do what God wants. Our problem, of course, is pride. It is our love of self which stands in the way. Unfortunately, we think that we know better than God. This is not only a grave insult to God, but sheer folly. How can we imagine that we know better than God? Just a few minutes' reflection, and we realise how pitiful is our knowledge. In the history of philosophy in Europe, in the time of the Enlightenment, quite a lot of philosophers, on becoming aware that science had an explanation for some of the problems of the universe which hitherto they had found hard to understand and had simply invoked God as the answer, jettisoned God and his wisdom, having concluded science had an answer for everything. In this, I think the first thing to put right is this absurd notion that human knowledge has an answer to everything, when we know very, very little. Furthermore, people have, in my opinion, by and large, lost their admiration for all God's beautiful works, and really have lost their appreciation of the beauty of his creation. On top of that there is a silly pride and vanity abroad which makes scientists come out with absurd and clearly false hypotheses claiming a new discovery which shows their intelligence in good light, with the implication that they are wiser than God. In all this, men fail to give God the credit for all the wonderful works of the world. How important it is to have the virtue of humility especially in the area of science. The science worker should keep on telling himself and God, if he happens to light upon some understanding of God's work of creation, how wonderful you are, O Lord, in all your works!

PUBLIC LIFE

WE COULD SAY THAT OUR Lord's Public Life, when he manifests his identity as the Chosen One of God, the promised Messiah, began with the first miracle at Cana of Galilee, when he changed the water into wine. However, although this shows Our Lord to be special and indeed, to be God, revealing himself to the world, nevertheless, we have to say, along with the first Mystery of Light of the Holy Rosary, that it was at the Baptism of Our Lord in the Jordan, by St John the Baptist, that Our Lord was clearly identified.

As we remember, when Our Lord was being baptised, a voice came from Heaven, which was obviously that of God the Father, *'This is my beloved Son, in whom I am well pleased' (Mt 17:5)*, and at the same time a dove was seen which was the Holy Spirit. So, not only was Our Lord identified as the Son of God, but the Holy Spirit as well, the Blessed Trinity. All revealed from the very start of Our Lord's Public Life.

But that is not all that is revealed. This is the beginning of God's revelation in the Person of Jesus Christ, God made man. At this stage, I feel it is very important to explain, if I have not done so already, the difference between the predicamental order and the transcendental order. This is typical scholastic philosophy. The predicamental order is our order as created by God, and there is a vast difference between our order or condition, as opposed to the transcendental order, to which God belongs. The distinction arises, you may remember when in ordinary language we say something like: Peter is a man. Now, if we were to say 'Peter is...' without finishing the sentence, and were to speculate, what is going to follow? Is Peter a man, or possibly a dog, or a little lamb, we realise that of all the possible predicates, once we have declared he is a man we have thereby eliminated all the other possible predicates. By pronouncing Peter's identity with the predicament 'man' I have thereby excluded all the other predicaments. 'Predicament' therefore signifies limitation. We belong to the predicamental order, and by identifying any predicament we have simultaneously pointed to something limited. Not all statements, however, necessarily indicate limitation. If, for example, I say, 'Peter is a man' is true; 'Peter is sad' is also true, 'The water is cold', 'The sky is blue' are also true, we realise that they all share in being true, the truth is an attribute which transcends the limitation of the predicamental order, to which all the statements belong. This was the discovery of Plato, via Socrates - the transcendental order or order of ideas as he called it. Aristotle, for his part, was more inclined to keep to the material universe, identified the predicaments, which he called categories as ten possible ways in which predication was possible, some predicates, identified a thing, substance, others different qualities, like a colour, hardness, or others put things in a place, 'where' or in time 'when' or relationship with others, position etc.

But why have I gone to the bother of inflicting another philosophy lesson on you? The answer is - to answer the question of who and what Our Lord is. Jesus Christ is God made man. In the Hidden Life, Jesus is clearly Man, but now he is God made Man. He is both God and Man, and belongs to both the Transcendental Order and the Predicamental Order. Well it has been my belief - practically the whole of what I might call my teaching life, to say that your understanding of Jesus Christ will fall short, if you do not appreciate this philosophical distinction. You see the point is that Jesus Christ, our Saviour, saved us working in and through the predicamental order. The Incarnation is the doctrine that tells us that the Second Person of the Blessed Trinity, enjoying, so-to-speak, the divine nature, took to himself, a human nature, from the womb of the Blessed Virgin Mary: he became man. And as man, he entered the predicamental order, with all its limitations. What is clear from our theology is that we were redeemed by the life, sufferings and death of Christ on the Cross, that is, in his human nature. The acceptability of Christ's actions to God the Father, in atonement of our sins, is because of <u>who</u> Our Lord is, God's beloved Son, but the actions are, as-it-were, our actions, belonging to the predicamental order. But then again, because Our Lord is redeeming us through his human nature, it means our access to the effects of the work of redemption is achieved through our relationship with Our Lord's Humanity.

When Our Lord was baptised and the Holy Spirit descended upon him, in St Luke's Gospel, it says and *'by the Spirit he was led out into the wilderness...' (Mt 4:1)*. This is where, for our sake, Jesus was tempted by the Devil and suffered hunger and thirst. And then we find him in the Synagogue in Nazareth, telling them that the words of Isaiah are fulfilled in himself and that he has been anointed and sent out to preach the Gospel to the poor. And from that moment on Our Lord spends himself in reaching out to people. We read a little later on in St Luke's Gospel that having reached a certain place the people wanted him to stay there with them, but he said he had to go and preach in other places too. The question is now, did he need to do this? And St John Chrysostom says 'no'. The reason why he says this is twofold: one reason is because he is God and God is everywhere, and the second reason is that just as people had already followed him, he could have stayed anywhere and the crowds would have followed him. So then, why did Our Lord move around so much? I have never been to the Holy Land, but some people I knew once told me on returning from a pilgrimage, said they had been on a coach tour of all the places Our Lord had been to and despite the fact they were in a coach, said they totally exhausted and Our Lord went to all these places on foot! So again, I ask why? And the answer as before is, *'actio Christi fuit nostra instructio'* (*'the action of Christ was to show us what we should do'*). This puts me in mind of what the Father said to Michael Richards, the first member of Opus Dei in England. He said that most of the money we would spend in Opus Dei would be on travel.

However, there is in fact another reason, which we can call 'body language'. Our Lord was driven by the Spirit into the desert, anointed with the Spirit, and then led by the Spirit to reach out to as many souls as possible, because of his love for souls. In the activity of Christ, we are seeing the effects of his burning love for souls. And why is this? Because he belongs to the predicamental order. It is true that in his divinity he could act upon each soul as his Lord and God, and influence souls through his Spirit, but the work of redemption is brought about through the action of his holy humanity and in his humanity he is confined to the predicamental order. He was living in a clearly defined part of the world – Palestine - and at a particular moment in history, two thousand years ago. He expresses through his ceaseless activity, his burning concern to reach out to as many souls as possible in the time he spent on earth. But, using his intelligence, and working in a very human way, he gathered around him a group of disciples, both men and women, who would undertake to be his loudspeakers, to act on his behalf. That is why he told them: Go out and teach all nations. Sometimes, it seems to me that there are people who think that the Church is just a happy thought, a means of comfort and help in living together, forgetting that the principal reason for its existence is to carry out apostolate and continue the work of Redemption. That is why when we consider the importance of imitating Jesus Christ, we not only try to copy all his many virtues, but also enter into that exquisite mind and that loving Heart and try to carry out his saving work with as many souls as we can. It is clearly not enough just to imitate the Sacred Humanity in the externals but to be imbued with the same fire and zeal in Christ's soul. We are reminded of this in *The Forge*, no.1:

> *'We are children of God, bearers of the only flame that can light up the paths of the earth for souls, the only brightness which can never be darkened, dimmed or over-shadowed.*
>
> *The Lord uses us as torches, to make that light shine out. Much depends on us; if we respond many people will remain in darkness no longer, but will walk instead along paths that lead to eternal life.'*

In all of this we have to remind ourselves that because Our Lord has redeemed us through his body, through his holy humanity, his calling us to be co-redeemers is not an optional extra, simply a good idea, but a vital necessity if we are to help him to save souls. This distinction between the predicamental order and the transcendental order brings home to us the awareness that Our Lord has real need of us. Of course, any one person is dispensable but together as the Church, we are all needed. This lends force to the obligation we have to carry out apostolate. In turn our doctrine - the things we say to people - has to be straight and true. It is Christ's doctrine and truth we have to put over, not our own ideas.

However, I think it is very important to reflect once more on the great need we have to carry out an intense apostolate. When St Teresa of Avila had experienced the terrible vision of Hell, which left her trembling with fright she said:

> 'It was that vision which filled me with the very great distress which I feel at the sight of so many lost souls, especially of the Lutherans, for they were once members of the Church by Baptism, and also gave me the most vehement desires for the salvation of souls; for certainly I believe that, to save even one from those overwhelming torments, I would willingly endure many deaths. If here on earth we see one whom we especially love in great trouble or pain, our very nature seems to bid us to compassionate him; and if those pains be great, we are troubled ourselves. What then, must it be to see a soul in danger of pain, the most grievous of all pains, forever? Who can endure it? It is a thought no heart can bear without great anguish. Here we know that pain ends with life at last, and that there are limits to it; yet the sight of it moves our compassion so greatly. That other pain has no ending. I do not know how we can be calm, when we see Satan carry off so many souls daily' (Chapter 32 in her 'Life').

APOSTOLATE IN THE FAMILY

We have mentioned the importance of communicating true doctrine. When it comes to the family and friends, it seems to me that it is a question of love. Apostolate takes the form of love in the intimacy of the home. It is vital for the Christian to demonstrate towards the other members of the family the love of Christ. For if we do not communicate love to our nearest and dearest, who are we to communicate it to?

In particular, the children in a family, feed not only on milk, but the milk of human kindness. Broken up families leave the children not only broken up hearts, but broken up lives. Children who have never enjoyed the warmth and love of their own parents are often fractious and difficult to control. Sometimes, it happens that the man and wife allow their differences to spill over to the detriment of the children. So, from the beginning of their lives the children reflect the bitterness of the selfishness of their parents. St Josemaría acknowledged that parents would almost inevitably have their quarrels and even rows, but they should keep this from their offspring. Otherwise, the children are bound to take sides. Either one or the other is in the wrong. Either Daddy is a monster oppressing Mummy or Mum is a shrew constantly provoking him to anger! What are they to do? Once the children have been exposed to the manifestation of the differences it is extremely hard to avoid disastrous consequences. For parents reading this I hope they take note and make a good examination of conscience. How would it have been in the Holy Family of Jesus Mary and Joseph? True apostolate with friends, as in the family, is based on trust. Many a time when asked which human virtue was the most important, St Josemaria often replied loyalty (instead of sincerity) because this is the human basis of success both in the family and in society as a whole. Wars, quarrels mutual difficulties start out with suspicions. I remember a marriage case in which the husband having had extra work to do, called in at a public house for a drink, to calm down before going home. His wife, however, began to suspect his lateness was due to his interest in other women so she called in at the public house, discovered that one of the barmaids was pretty, put two and two together and made five, and went off and committed adultery in another town, saying 'I too can play at that game', after which the husband left his wife and they divorced!

Marriage is based on trust, as is every friendship and the whole of society. Now, if we trust our friends, we will communicate our most intimate knowledge of our life and even our problems. It will be a mutual communication. If we are in the role of an apostle, we will be encouraged to urge our friend to share in our life of piety and love for God and Our Lady.

This can lead to greater things. The person who is our friend may be converted into a great apostle of Jesus Christ. It is easy to see this in the early part of the Gospel. Andrew and John were the first to discover Jesus, John went and told his brother, James, Andrew told his brother Simon, whom Our Lord renamed Peter, and also his friend, Philip who in turn found Nathanael. This the apostolate of friendship and trust.

On retreats I have sometimes put it to the group attending, about twenty: supposing that everyone of us here, converts one more person by the end of the year, filling him with the determination to be a lively apostle who will do the same with a friend of his the following year and all do the same. Given that there are some five or six thousand million souls in the world, how long would it take to convert the whole world into fervent Christians? The answer: twenty years. Obviously, I have not worked out the mathematical exponential series with any accuracy, but I remember once a gentleman who was good at maths on a retreat I gave actually did do the calculation and came up with the answer: 28.5 years, on the basis that there were in fact on that retreat sixteen people in the oratory! The problem lies with us. Do I really carry out an effective apostolate? This is answered in a certain fashion by a point in *The Way*, 761:

> 'Free man, subject yourself to voluntary servitude so that Jesus will not have to say of you what we are told he said of others to Saint Teresa: 'Teresa, I wanted it, but men did not'.

PASTORAL WORK OF A PRIEST

It has occurred to me that some readers might be priests so I thought it might be in order to make some suggestions which could be of use. A priest's vocation consists in being endowed with a certain kind of power which he received at the laying on of hands by the Bishop. With ordination the priestly soul which he already received on being baptised is enhanced. The Dogmatic Constitution on the Church tells us in paragraph 10:

> 'There is an essential difference between the faithful's priesthood in common and the priesthood of the ministry or the hierarchy, and not just a difference of degree. Nevertheless, there is an ordered relation between them: one and the other has its special way of sharing the single priesthood of Christ. The priest, by the sacred power that he enjoys, is responsible for the formation and the government of the priestly people; in the person of Christ he makes the eucharistic sacrifice and offers it in the name of the whole of God's people. The faithful, in virtue of their royal priesthood, concur in the offering of the Eucharist, and they practise their priesthood in the reception of the sacraments, in prayer and thanksgiving, the witness of a holy life, self-denial and active charity'.

We should be careful to note that the principal characteristic of the ministerial priest is the sacred power he enjoys. His fundamental role, therefore, consists in exercising this power. On the last day Our Lord is going to ask him how he used this specific talent which he had received. Did he, as a good shepherd feed his flock with the Bread of Life? How did he celebrate the Holy Sacrifice of the Mass and ensure that the Liturgy was conducted in a way that invited the faithful to participate fruitfully? Did he make himself available for people to receive the Sacrament of Penance easily; did he visit the sick and ensure that the dying were anointed before it was too late? I do not I need go on, because it will occur to any priest's conscience to respond. The priest is called upon to live a life of sacrifice; like his Master he should be ready to lay it down for the sake of his flock, Christ's flock. Meanwhile, we all have a priestly soul. When we survey the world, we must be struck by the multitude of souls who are like sheep without a shepherd. I remember walking through one of the geriatric wards in Withington Hospital in Manchester, which has sadly been demolished since, so that the Manchester Royal Infirmary could be expanded. I was moved to see so many elderly people in various postures in their beds, clearly feeling distressed, and I said to myself, they do not know why they are here, they do not know why they are suffering why they are in pain. It put me in mind of the point in *The Forge*, no. 928:

> 'My child, offer him even the sorrows and sufferings of other people'.

As we go about our lives, we carry with us our priestly soul which is anxious to imitate Jesus Christ in carrying the burdens of the sins and sorrows of the people around.

This is brought out by St Josemaría in another point, this time from *The Way*, no. 866:

> 'Good child: offer him the work of those labourers who do not know him; offer him the natural joy of those poor little ones who are brought up in pagan schools'.

This applies to every good apostolic Christian, but the priest is especially bound by the duty of speaking clearly, when the occasion warrants it; of reminding people of God's commandments; for if the priest does not who will? Sometimes when I have spoken to priests I have come to the conclusion that sadly, on occasions, they have failed to remind married people of responsibilities they may find hard to carry out, correcting their children; practising chastity; avoiding the use of artificial contraceptives; speaking about the judgment and the existence of Hell. There is obviously no need to go on and on about it; but these difficult subjects have to be brought to people's attention. When laypeople carry out their personal apostolate in conversation with their friends, they should not be afraid to touch on subjects which we tend to avoid.

As we close this section it is appropriate to remember that the obligation to carry out apostolate belongs to every single member of the Church, young or old, sick or healthy. We are reminded of this in the Decree on the Apostolate of the Laity, Chapter I:

> 'The Church came into existence to make all men sharers of a saving redemption. To accomplish this, she enlarges the kingdom of Christ, which gives glory to God the

Father, until it embraces the whole earth. So, through men's efforts the whole world will, in all reality, be concentrated on Christ. Every effort, then, of the Mystical Body which is directed to this purpose, deserves to be called an apostolic work; for here we have the Church carrying on her apostolate in many different ways and through every one of her members. The summons to follow Christ is of its very nature also a summons to be an apostle. In the structure of a living organism none of the organs is simply inert; in sharing the vitality of the organism, they share also its activity. So also in the body of Christ, which the Church is, the whole body 'according to the operation in the measure of every part, maketh increase of the body (Eph 4: 16). In fact, the organs of this body are so interconnected and fitted together (cf. Eph 4:16) that an organ which does not function according to its capacity and so build up the body, cannot be said to benefit either the Church or itself'.

With that long quotation, it is time to move on to the end of Our Lord's life.

THE LAST SUPPER: THE NEW COMMANDMENT

THERE WERE TWO THINGS OUR Lord wanted to do during the Last Supper he spent with his disciples: one was to give them his Commandment of love, and the other His Body and Blood. One was his last will and testament as the saying goes, the other, the wherewithal to carry it out. It is in the Gospel of St John that we read the words of the New Commandment:

> *'I have a new commandment to give you, that you are to love one another; that your love for one another is to be like the love I have borne you. The mark by which all men will know you for my disciples will be the love you bear one another'* (Jn 13:34).

On the face of it, I am sure the disciples understood this to mean that they were to show their fellow disciples the same tenderness and affection which Jesus had shown towards each one of them, that is, a human love. And this would fit in very well with the secondary injunction, that this would be a sign of discipleship. I found that out for myself when I was with St Josemaría, for he loved me in such a way that I found myself saying to myself, if an ordinary human being can show so much love and affection as this man has to me, what must it have been like to have known Jesus and his love? I found myself uplifted on several occasions. Sometimes I had been down in the dumps, mainly on account of failing oral examinations of the philosophy courses we had been following. The main excuse I had was that I was unable to speak in my native tongue,

English, during the exams. As a consequence, I had failed a considerable number. And then, the bell sounded: the signal that St Josemaría was in the soggiorno (Italian for sitting-room) and there would be a get-together with him very shortly! What joy! I forgot my troubles and woes, - how he made us forget these earthly thoughts - it wasn't that he expounded lots of pious invocations, but he made observations about life and the world in general in a supernatural way. So much so that you felt you were in a different world. God's world. He was clearly teaching us to be supernatural in outlook like himself, and we would continue to pass this idea on to our friends and acquaintances in the course of time in later life.

However, when you examine the words of Jesus Christ and analyse what he has just said, *'love one another as I have loved you'* (Jn 13:34), you have to acknowledge that it is utterly and completely impossible. Jesus Christ is God, made man, true, but God nevertheless, so how can I possibly love in the same way, as if I were God? That is why I started by saying that in the Last Supper, Jesus gave us the commandment and then the wherewithal to fulfil it, since the Holy Eucharist endows us with the god-like power of the supernatural life. Of course, at this stage in the proceedings the apostles had not really any idea, of either implication, first, that they were expected to love like God, and second, that they were be enabled to do so with the Holy Eucharist.

My question is, of course, do the Christians of today realise these implications? Do they realise that when they are called by Jesus Christ to love like him, they have to be endowed with the supernatural virtue of charity in order to be able to do it? And do they realise that the Holy Eucharist contains the Body, Blood, Soul and Divinity of Jesus Christ and that this Sacrament carries with it the supernatural grace and the supernatural virtues of Faith, Hope and Charity that are infused into the soul on receiving this august Sacrament? My feeling is that they do not. But then, you who I confidently hope and trust, are reflecting on these truths, will take them to heart, put them into practice, and then, God willing, pass them on to others.

But what does it mean, really, to love others as Jesus has loved us? Do we remember how this passage of St John's Gospel began? It began, if you remember, with Our Lord, setting his robe aside, kneeling down, and washing the feet of his disciples. Here a word of explanation is clearly in order, for nowadays people don't go around in general with rope sandals on their feet and walk dusty roads like those of Palestine of long ago. So, washing one's feet after a journey, is not really required. What are we left with? Do we just set the whole thing aside saying the Gospel is totally out of date and consequently, irrelevant? Of course not. Our Lord is performing a simple act of service, which demands adopting the role of a humble servant, and an action of sacrifice and generosity. When he had sat down again, Jesus then said:

> 'Do you understand what it is I have done to you? You hail me as the Master, and the Lord; and you are right, it is what I am. Why then if I have washed your feet, I who am the Master and the Lord, you in your turn ought to wash each other's feet; I have been setting you an example, which will teach you in your turn to do what I have done for you' (Jn 13:14).

This part of the Gospel is reminiscent of St Matthew's Gospel, Chapter 23, where he points out that he does not want them to be like the Scribes and Pharisees who have taken it upon themselves to be like Moses and guide the people. But instead of being humble and serving others they have made use of their exalted position to further their own power and situation and be admired and applauded. So, Jesus is afraid they will become proud and conceited, when he has gone, and they have taken over his role of guiding the people. He wants them humble; he does not want them to abuse their new found authority and if they become shepherds of the flock, he wants them to be good shepherds who lay down their life for the sheep.

So how does that square with the way we behave? Are we good shepherds ready for sacrifice, or rather do we impose on others? If so, we shall have to beg forgiveness of God and indeed make amends. It is not easy if we have been given a position of authority, because it easily goes to our head. We begin to think we are important people and God had no alternative but to choose us. I always think of those words which we find in the story of St Margaret Mary Alocoque. On one of the last occasions when Jesus appeared to the Saint, he said to her, in words similar to these, '*Oh, by the way Margaret, in case you might be tempted to think you were special in some way, remember that when I was looking for someone to be my apostle of the Sacred Heart, I went round the world in search of someone more miserable and wretched than you, and on failing to find anyone, I chose you*'! I wonder what she thought? Knowing her - at least as she is described in the biographies - she will have taken it in her stride and accepted it in her humility.

Turning once more to the aspect of charity. We also need to reflect on how well we carry out the New Commandment. St Josemaría, as we know, tells us that the adjective '*new*', applies to this commandment, for the simple reason that it applies because the Commandment is a like a pair of new shoes that no one has tried on yet and that is why it is *new*. Do we in fact love others as Jesus has loved us? He loves us with an infinite, all-embracing love; with all our faults and failings, and with an earnest desire to see us improve and work towards sanctity. Many, including Christians, look upon others instead in a vengeful way if they have suffered some humiliation at their hands, and even take steps to get their own back.

Reflections like these should lead us to make resolutions to look upon others with kindness and tenderness, wanting to see even people who do us wrong, change and strive for holiness and ultimately be rewarded with happiness in heaven. Many years after St Josemaría had been calumniated and persecuted by certain priests who treated him as a heretic, he prayed for them in the Holy Sacrifice of the Mass long after they had died.

THE HOLY EUCHARIST

After Jesus had washed his disciples' feet, he turned to the other important thing he wanted to do before his Passion: the institution of the Holy Eucharist. He is reported in St Luke's Gospel, with very profound and touching words, '*desiderio desideravi*' - '*I have longed and longed to share this Paschal Meal with you before my passion*' (Lk 22:15).

These words express the essence of the Eucharist. This is the manifestation of Our Lord's love for each one of us. To die and then to rise for us, provides the grace of the Redemption for one and all, but the grace of the Redemption has to be applied to each one, singly, as it was when Jesus went around Palestine, curing the sick, *'singulis manus imponens'* (*'placing his hands on each one'*) (Lk 4:40). The grace for all is there, as the Pool of Bethsaida was there for anyone who bathed in it, but not everyone managed to get into the Pool as is recorded in St John's Gospel, Chapter Five. So, the grace of the Sacrament of the Holy Eucharist is available for all who make the effort to make themselves worthy of so great a grace. God wants all to be saved. This is shown not only by St Paul's words to Timothy *'since it is his will that all men should be saved...'* (1 Tim 2:4), but by the parable of the Wedding Feast where he orders his servants to go out into the highways and byways, but at the same time, only those persons can partake of the banquet who are properly dressed: in other words in a state of grace.

When St Josemaría was in Chile in 1974, on one occasion, I think it was in the headquarters of Opus Dei in Santiago, he gave a homily, just before distributing Holy Communion. Before the Second Vatican Council it was traditional for the priest to give a short homily immediately before giving Holy Communion to the faithful. I must say I never dared do it, although I knew St Josemaría had done it on numerous occasions. Anyway, in Chile, he spoke wanting to prepare his sons and tell them how to receive Our Lord, and he said:

> *'My sons, the Lord is now about to enter into your hearts. So now at this early time of the morning, I like to make, and I would like you to make, an act of clear, explicit faith: Lord, I believe it is You, hidden in the bread. I believe it is you, Jesus of Nazareth, the one at the wedding feast of Cana; the one who cured the lepers, who raised the dead, the one who suffered the Passion and died on the Cross, who rose on the third day. I know that you are here, really, truly and substantially present, with your Body, with your Blood, with your Soul, and with your divinity.*
>
> *It is good that we begin in this way. Afterwards, each one of you can do his own thanksgiving. For myself, I tell*

> him that I don't know what has possessed him to come to this dust-bin of my heart. Once again, he has wanted to humble himself.
>
> It was a great humiliation to take flesh of a slave, but to come here......And he also enters your hearts too, my sons! He comes as a doctor, as a father, as a teacher, as food, as strength, as companion and friend. Treat him as you like, but treat him well for me! But don't just thank him for only a few minutes: thank him all through the day! A word of gratitude because you have received him into your breast. A word of gratitude in the hope that tomorrow you will have him once more within you, in spite of our unworthiness.
>
> Invoke Our Lady, his Mother and our Mother. Invoke the Patriarch St Joseph. We are now in our family; already we find ourselves in the intimacy of our home, and we can speak about whatever we like: each one of his things; and all of us together, of our things, for we are an immense family, with so many needs both material and spiritual, all of them directed, ... these needs and these efforts to give him glory, to spread his kingdom in the world...'.

These words end on a note of petition. What better opportunity to ask Our Lord for all his graces? But this should make us think. But what about you Lord, I know that you have come to satisfy my needs, to be my crook and my staff to be my consolation and strength. Do you find love and gratitude in me?

Now, to change the subject slightly. We have been considering so far, the Holy Eucharist as a Sacrament. Now we have to look at it as a Sacrifice. We know that the Holy Eucharist is an enactment of the Cross. Not everyone was able to stand with Our Lady at the foot of the Cross, and yet through the Mass they are enabled to do this. The reason is because the celebration of the Holy Mass is a re-presentation of the Cross. So, this then places a serious obligation on us if we are to assist at Mass properly, for we have to have the same disposition we should have had if we were at the foot of the Cross. But what do we find? Instead of concentrating on Our Lord's love and generosity - which he lived during his Passion -we find ourselves distracted, our thoughts anywhere and everywhere. It is clear we should invoke our Guardian Angel and (if you are a priest) your Ministerial Archangel, to keep focused on God, and making sure our offering is sincere and true. It means we should remember, as St Josemaría used to do, that Our Lady is present with us at the altar, and no doubt, St Joseph too, enabling us to offer ourselves and all our sacrifices to our heavenly Father. Another problem then arises, which is pointed out by Father Eugene Boylan, in one of his wonderful books, which is that we approach the altar with our poor offerings, and present them to Our Lord, and he says to us, 'but, my son, are you thinking of making this offering to God, our loving Father? But you can't for it isn't worthy of him, here, give it to me', and he takes it in <u>his holy and venerable hands</u> (Roman Canon) and sanctifies our offering uniting it with his supreme sacrifice of his suffering and death, and offers it all to his heavenly Father. And so, we see how the Holy Sacrifice of the Mass enhances our poor offerings and they are then transformed into a supreme Sacrifice to God.

Finally, we find in the works of St Peter Eymard words which were repeated constantly by St Josemaría, *'All our works must converge towards Communion as towards their end and flow from it as from its source. The Mass has to be the centre and the root of our interior life. We need to remember the Mass all through the day, thanking God for the Mass celebrated and preparing for the Mass to come. In this way all our deeds, words and works are sanctified, elevated as loving praise to God and converted into an instrument of apostolate'.*

THE PASSION AND DEATH OF OUR LORD JESUS CHRIST

MEDITATING ON THE PASSION AND Death of Our Lord is mainly about retrospect or retroactive prayer and sacrifice. Our Lord suffered and died for us and we always have to keep this in mind when we meditate on his sufferings. Like St Alphonsus we have to say to ourselves, as we contemplate the scenes, '*He did it all for me*'.

As a consequence, I must try to alleviate his sufferings by our own sacrifices. As St Josemaría often repeated: '**love is repaid with love**'.

When Our Lord had sung a hymn, as it says in the Gospel, he went out from the Upper Room, and led his disciples into the garden of Gethsemane, where they could be alone and undisturbed. This is another example of what we mentioned earlier on about how Our Lord habitually sought a quiet place for prayer. On this occasion, he not only took his disciples into this remote place, but went further, taking just Peter, James and John, who had witnessed his transfiguration to prepare them precisely for this, his prayer in the garden. Then he separated himself still further from them and fell on his face. And what was it he was doing? He was crying, weeping bitterly over us and our sins. He was not only overcome with sorrow for our sins, but the sins of the whole world. This is the beginning of the retrospect, and I should have added the anticipation of all the sins of people yet to come, and added to his burden. I hope I mentioned, in fact I am sure I did mention the witness of Don Julian Herranz, (Don Julian Herranz is a Cardinal who used to be the President of the Council for the Interpretation of Texts and who lived with St Josemaría for many years) who spoke about how, when Jesus spoke to the people of his time, being God, and transcending time, he was also speaking to all of us, who live at different periods of history. Well, this is also true of Our Lord's sufferings and his death on the Cross which apply to all souls throughout history. St. John Henry, Cardinal Newman records the whole event in his *'Discourses to Mixed Congregations: The Mental Sufferings of Our Lord in his Passion'*:

> *'And now, my brethren, what was it He had to bear, when he thus opened upon his soul the torrent of this predestined pain? Alas! He had to bear what is well known to us, what is familiar to us, but what to him was woe unutterable. He had to bear that which is so easy a thing to us, so natural, so welcome, that we cannot conceive of it as a great endurance, but which to him had the scent and the poison of death. He had, my dear brethren, to bear the weight of sin; He had to bear our sins; He had to bear the sins of the whole world. Sin is an easy thing to us; we think little of it; we cannot bring our imagination to believe that it deserves retribution, and, when even in this world punishments follow upon it, we explain them away or turn our minds from them. But consider what sin is in itself; it is rebellion against God; it is a traitor's act who aims at the overthrow and death of his sovereign: it is that, if I may use a strong expression, which, could the Divine Governor of the world cease to be, would be sufficient to bring it about. Sin is the mortal enemy of the All-holy so that He and it cannot be together; and as the All-holy drives it from his presence into the outer darkness, so, if God could be less than God, it is sin that would have power to make Him less. And here, observe, my brethren, that when once Almighty Love, by taking flesh, entered this created system, and submitted himself to its laws, then forthwith this antagonist of good and truth, taking advantage of the opportunity, flew at that flesh which He had taken, and fixed on it, and was its death. The envy of the Pharisees, the treachery of Judas, and the madness of the people, were but the instrument*

or the expression of the enmity which sin felt towards Eternal Purity as soon as, in infinite mercy towards men, He put Himself within its reach. Sin could not touch His Divine Majesty; but it could assail Him in that way in which He allowed Himself to be assailed, that is, through the medium of His humanity. And in the issue, in the death of God incarnate, you are but taught, my brethren, what sin is in itself, and what it was which then was falling, in its hour and its strength, upon His human nature, when He allowed that nature to be so filled with horror and dismay at the very anticipation.

There, then, in that most awful hour, knelt the Saviour of the world, putting off the defences of His divinity, dismissing His reluctant Angels, who in myriads were ready at His call, and opening His arms, baring His breast, sinless as He was, to the assault of His foe, -of a foe whose breath was a pestilence and whose embrace was an agony. There He knelt, motionless and still, while the vile and horrible fiend clad His spirit in a robe steeped in all that is hateful and heinous in human crime, which clung close round His heart, and filled his conscience, and found its way into every sense and pore of His mind, and spread over Him a moral leprosy, till He almost felt Himself to be that which He never could be, and which His foe would fain have made Him. Oh, the horror, when He looked, and did not know Himself, and felt as a foul and loath-some sinner, from His vivid perception of that mass of corruption which poured over His head and ran down even to the skirts of His garments! Oh, the distraction, when He found His eyes, and feet, and lips, and heart, as if the members of the Evil One, and not of God! Are these the hands of the Immaculate Lamb of God, once innocent, but now red with ten thousand barbarous deeds of blood? Are these His lips, not uttering prayer, and praise, and holy blessings, but as if defiled with oaths, and blasphemies, and doctrines of devils? Or

His eyes, profaned as they are by all the evil visions and idolatrous fascinations for which men have abandoned their adorable Creator? And His ears, they ring with the sounds of revelry and strife; and His heart is frozen with avarice, and cruelty and unbelief; and His very memory is laden with every sin which has been committed since the fall, in all the regions of the earth, with the pride of the old giants, and the lusts of the five cities, and the obduracy of Egypt, and the ambition of Babel, and the unthankfulness and scorn of Israel. Oh, who does not know the misery of a haunting thought which comes again and again, in spite of rejection, to annoy, if it cannot seduce? Or of some odious and sickening imagination, in no sense one's own, but forced upon the mind from without? Or of evil knowledge, gained with or without a man's fault; but which he gives a great price to be rid of at once and forever? And adversaries such as these gather around Thee, Blessed Lord, in millions now; they come in troops more numerous than the locust or the palmer-worm, or the plagues of hail, and flies, and frogs, which were sent against Pharaoh. Of the living and of the dead and of the as yet unborn, of the lost and of the saved, of Thy people and of strangers, of sinners and of saints, all sins are there. Thy dearest are there, Thy saints and Thy chosen are upon Thee; Thy three apostles, Peter and James, and John, but not as comforters as accusers, like the friends of Job, 'sprinkling dust towards heaven', and heaping curses on Thy head. All are there but one, one only is not there, one only; for she who had no part in sin, she only could console Thee, and therefore she is not nigh. She will be near Thee on the Cross, she is separated from Thee in the Garden. She has been Thy companion and confidant through Thy life, she interchanged with Thee the pure thoughts and holy meditations of thirty years; but her virgin ear may not take in, nor may her immaculate heart conceive, what now is in vision before Thee. None is equal to the weight but God; sometimes before Thy saints Thou has brought the image of a single sin, as it appears in the light of Thy countenance, or of venial sins, not mortal; and they have told us that the sight did all but kill them, nay, would have killed them, had it not been instantly withdrawn. The Mother of God, for all her sanctity, nay, by reason of it, could not have borne even one brood of that innumerable progeny of Satan which now compass Thee about. It is the long history of a world, and God alone can bear the load of it. Hopes blighted, vows broken, lights quenched, warnings scorned, opportunities lost, the innocent betrayed, the young hardened, the penitent relapsing, the just overcome, the aged failing; the sophistry of misbelief, wilfulness of passion, the obduracy of pride, the tyranny of habit, the canker of remorse, the wasting fever of care, the anguish of shame, the pining of disappointment, the sickness of despair, such cruel, such pitiable spectacles, such heart-rending, revolting, detestable, maddening scenes; nay, the haggard faces, the convulsed lips, the flushed cheek, the hard brow of the willing slaves of evil, they are all before Him now; they are upon Him and which has inhabited His soul since the moment of His conception. They are upon Him, they are all but His own; He cries to His Father as if He were a criminal, not the victim; His agony takes the form of guilt and compunction. He is doing penance, He is making Confession, He is exercising contrition, with a reality and a virtue infinitely greater than that of all the saints and penitents together; for He is the One Victim for us all, the sole Satisfaction, the real Penitent, all but the real sinner.'

From all this long quotation which enables us to appreciate the agony Our Lord endured, we surely should be moved to alleviate Our Lord's suffering by refraining from adding to His burden, and responding to his call to us to watch and pray.

When Our Lord rose from his prayer, he seemed to be himself again, dignified and composed. We cannot know what his feelings were when Judas kissed him on the cheek to betray him to the soldiers. Nevertheless, while we meditate on his suffering, we need to keep on trying to appreciate his innermost thoughts. As St John Henry Newman says, the only one who can console him properly is Our Lady; but she also suffers with him during the following hours of pain. It is impossible to describe all that Our Lord suffered, so each one should reflect on the different scenes and perhaps make use of the sequence we follow in The Way of the Cross. We find included in the book, *The Way of the Cross* by St Josemaría, a considerable number of extra considerations which can help us to enter into the scenes. One of these, following the eighth station says:

> '*The saints, you tell me, would burst into tears of sorrow at the thought of the Passion of Our Lord. Whereas I…*
> *Perhaps that is because you and I witness the scenes, but do not 'live' them'. (Way of the Cross, 8th Station)*

One of the events which occurred on The Way of the Cross, which lends itself to this application is when Our Lady, no doubt accompanied by St John, meets Our Lord on his way to Calvary. And what does she find? Our Lord, broken and beaten, covered with blood, and she exclaims (altering the words in St Luke's Gospel) 'my son, why have <u>they</u> treated you so?' So, we feel inclined to repeat her words, and we find the answer in the words of Chapter 53 of the Prophet Isaiah:

> '*He will watch this servant of his appear among us, unregarded as brushwood shoot, as a plant in waterless soil; no stateliness here, no majesty, no beauty, as we gaze upon him, to win our hearts. Nay, here is one despised, left out of all human reckoning; bowed with misery, and no stranger to weakness; how should we recognise that face? How should we take any account of him, a man so despised?*'

Yes, we will say. Who did all this to you, Jesus? And the text from Isaiah continues:

> 'Our weakness, and it was he carried the weight of it, our miseries, and it was he who bore them. A leper, so we thought of him, a man God had smitten and brought low; and all the while it was for our sins he was wounded, it was guilt of ours crushed him down; on him the punishment fell that brought us peace, by his bruises we were healed. Strayed sheep all of us, each following his own path; and God laid on his shoulders our guilt, the guilt of us all.'

Obviously, the time has come for us to pause and let this great truth sink in. We all have to acknowledge that it is our sins that have condemned Our Lord and caused him to suffer. First, then, an act of sorrow. Then the resolution to make amends. Sometimes we complain about our own sufferings and fail to realise that we suffer very little and that Our Lord has carried the burden on his own shoulders.

Throughout his Passion Our Lord himself utters not a word of complaint. He is totally innocent and yet he does not protest. In a letter written in Lyons 1674 after speaking to St Margaret Mary and learning about the Sacred Heart, and before going to London, St Claude de la Colombiere, wrote:

> 'The love of Our Lord's Heart was in no way diminished by the treason of Judas, the flight of the Apostles and the persecution of his enemies. Jesus was only grieved at the harm they did themselves; his sufferings helped to assuage his grief because he saw in them a remedy for the sins committed by his enemies. The Sacred Heart was full of the most tender love: there was no bitterness in it; neither the cruelty nor the injustice he received moved it to feelings other than those of compassion and affection.
>
> I turned to Mary and asked her to obtain for me the grace to imitate Our Lord's Heart. I saw how perfectly her heart copied His: she loved those who put her Son to death and offered Him to God the Father for them. This enkindled a very great love of virtue in my heart.

> *Oh Sacred Hearts of Jesus and Mary, truly worthy of possessing all hearts and of reigning over men and angels, you shall be my models; I will try to copy you. May my heart live always in the Hearts of Jesus and Mary, and may their hearts live in mine, so that I may never do anything that is not in accordance with them.'*

We have here the most wonderful explanation of what devotion to the Sacred Heart means. It means mercy. How necessary it is to follow the spirit of the merciful and all-forgiving heart of Jesus.

HE DID IT ALL FOR LOVE

In his book called '*Selva*' (which is the one directed to priests) St Alphonsus draws our attention to the same point St Thomas Aquinas makes in his hymn *Adoro te devote* where, in the last verse but one, he observes '*Cuius una stilla salvum facere, totum mundum quit ab omni scelere*'. ('*One drop of whose blood would be enough to cleanse the world of its guilt*'). Why then Lord, did you go through all that agony and go to the lengths of actually dying for us? St Alphonsus says it was to be able to ordain priests and ensure that there was a victim for the Sacrifice for the Mass.

At least, that is how I recall what he said. However, the usual answer is that Our Lord suffered and died to demonstrate his love for us. And as we have been meditating, he showed his love every step of the way and we derive great benefit from his ingenious way of manifesting his love for us. For he suffered both mentally and physically and in every one of his limbs and members. Such was the ingenuity of love, and thereby giving us ample opportunity to see his love manifested and all the virtues shown. I believe you can find in St Thomas the idea that during his Passion Our Lord showed forth every one of the Christian virtues. When I was in Rome, we used to have concerts from time to time on the big feast-days. As a rule, St Josemaría liked me to sing a song made popular by Perry Como: Hot-diggity. I must have sung that song for him a dozen times! However, I have to say it was not my favourite.

My choice would be what you would call a romantic ballad. And this type of song would have the advantage of being supernaturalised as St Josemaría often said. You could give the words a supernatural slant that could make the words apply to God. After all, holiness is really just a matter of loving God. One of these songs that I sang to St Josemaría in a concert was such a ballad, entitled: *'Love is a many-splendoured thing'*.

This has, I think, such a supernatural application. How can I explain it? We all remember how Jesus went to stay at Bethany which was where Martha, Mary and Lazarus lived. Martha was busy and distracted by waiting on many needs. She protested and asked Our Lord to get Mary to help her, and he told her: *'but only one thing is necessary'* (Lk 10: 42).

And so we ask: and what is this one thing? The answer of course is love. St Augustine says, somewhere: *'ama et fac quod vis';* *('love and do what you like')*. Obviously, we can't take that too literally. He means that provided love is the intention and driving-force you will be pleasing God. Love is a many-faceted thing or splendored thing if you like. It has many expressions, or ways of showing love to God. There is love which atones or makes reparation; there is a love which consoles him; a love which thanks him, which glorifies him, which praises him, which wants something, a love which sings to him. Our Lord is delighted with our love no matter what shape or form it takes. It can be work or rest, or even our sleep. As you probably know St Josemaría taught us to live a plan of life, which consists of different elements: morning offering, mental prayer, Holy Rosary, Angelus, Visit to the Blessed Sacrament and above all the Holy Sacrifice of the Mass. Interspersed among these more substantial practices of piety, we express our love for God, with aspirations, acts of sorrow, acts of thanksgiving, and so on. They are all aspects of love. It is not surprising to find that meditation on the Passion of Jesus evokes many different expressions of love. Another reason for meditation on it.

When Our Lord was about to expire, he had one more thing left to do to finish his work on earth and that was to bequeath his Mother to us. Fr Reginald Garrigou-Lagrange says:

> *'...it was on Calvary that Jesus proclaimed Mary our Mother, when He addressed to Mary the words: 'Woman,*

behold thy son' and to St John, (who personified all the redeemed) the words 'Behold thy Mother'.

Tradition has always understood the words in that sense: they do not refer to a grace peculiar to St John alone, but go beyond him to all who are to be regenerated by the Cross.

The words of the dying Saviour, like sacramental words, produce what they signify: in Mary's soul they produced a great increase of charity and of maternal love for us; in John a profound filial affection, full of reverence for the Mother of Mercy' (Garrigou-Lagrange, The Mother of the Saviour).

There is little more to be said. The great theologian is expressing what has always been the belief of true Christians, for how is it possible that if we love Jesus, we do not love his Mother? And Jesus has given her to us; she is the Mother of God and as St Josemaría used to say, our Mother also. This will lead us to remember Mary in our whole life. How those glances at her pictures help us to remember her and believe in her intercession? It is also the last manifestation of Our Lord's generosity. He has given us his life, and now he has given us his Mother and as man has nothing left.

THE GLORIOUS RESURRECTION OF OUR LORD JESUS CHRIST

WHEN OUR LORD DIED THERE was darkness all over the earth. So much so, it penetrated the minds and hearts of all of Our Lord's disciples, both men and women. They were filled with gloom and doom. Only one person retained a bright light in her heart, for, despite her intense sufferings with her Son, she had that burning faith and light in her soul, which has given her the title by which she is known when she rescues suffering souls from Purgatory: Star of the Sea. Pope St Pius X in his encyclical *Ad Diem Illum* says:

> 'In the midst of this deluge of evil the Virgin Most Merciful stands before us like a rainbow. She is the peace-maker between God and man: 'I will set my bow in the clouds, and it shall be a sign of a covenant between me and the earth.' When the last hour arrived 'there stood by the Cross of Jesus his Mother'
>
> She was not merely occupied in contemplating the cruel spectacle. She was also rejoicing that 'her only-begotten Son was being offered for the salvation of the human race. She suffered so much together with Him, that, if it had been possible, she would have been more than willing to bear all the torments that her Son suffered' Through this community of suffering and intention between Christ and Mary 'she merited to become in a

> *most noble manner the Reparatrix of the fallen world'.*
> *As a result of this, she is the Dispenser of all the gifts that*
> *Jesus acquired for us by His Death and Blood.'*

I have sometimes wondered why there is no mention of Our Lady in the texts of the Gospels regarding the Resurrection. There can only be one conclusion. This is similar to the one mentioned twice above regarding the actions of Jesus Christ: *'Actio Christi fuit nostra instructio',* ('*the action or actions of Christ were for our instruction'*). The things that Our Lord did were intended to help us and guide us and teach us. Our Lady had in a certain sense to keep out of the way. This was something the apostles had to learn by themselves. To begin with, despite the number times Our Lord had told them, *'but on the third day I will rise again' (Mt 27:63),* they simply did not believe Him, and did not believe in the Resurrection. And this was for our benefit; the benefit of you and me. If they had had Our Lady's faith, all these criticisms and false judgements about the Resurrection would have been accepted, because on the basis of their conviction that he would rise again, they would have engineered it. In fact, the other, hostile camp of the Scribes and Pharisees, seemed to have more faith than the disciples, or, at least a better memory of what Christ had said, so that they provided for this contingency by rolling the stone in place and surrounding the grave with soldiers to prevent the disciples from stealing the body. If we want any more proof of the attitude of the disciples, all we need to do is read St Luke's account of the two disciples running away from Jerusalem lamenting Our Lord's death and showing their sad disappointment. There is not even a hint of expectation that he would rise. This, then, means that when they did, they were able to give a simple straightforward witness of Our Lord's Resurrection. And then of course, when the penny dropped and it dawned on them that the Sun of Justice had risen, they were filled with joy. The two disciples who had previously argued that the day was far gone and the stranger should stay with them, when they discovered it was Our Lord, were so astonished they raced back to Jerusalem to tell the rest.

What I find most interesting about Our Lord's appearances to his disciples is that they are completely devoid of recrimination. Just imagine if you had been abandoned by your best friends and taken prisoner? Only one male apostle, St John, stood by him. So, when he appeared to them on Sunday, surely he would at least have chided them about their disloyalty, or, pointed out their chicken-heartedness, but not a word!

Instead, words of peace and consolation. It is as if they were the ones who had suffered cruelty and persecution. He is intent upon bringing peace and joy into their lives. So, then, this is what we must do; avoid all recrimination, always being positive and optimistic. This, of course, is the way to win souls for God, by letting them know they have a loving Saviour and also a loving Father.

The Resurrection of Jesus Christ is a fact of paramount importance. Our salvation hinges upon it. Some years ago, talking about the Work of Redemption to a couple of Catholic priests, it gradually became clear to me as the conversation progressed, they were of the opinion that when Our Lord died on the Cross, that was it, the work of redemption was now complete. At this, I blurted out, 'but that is Protestantism'. If Our Lord had not risen from the dead, he would have been just another man, well-endowed, better than everybody else, but just human. By rising from the dead Our Lord demonstrated, incontrovertibly, that he was God as well as man. But what about St Peter's sermons as recorded in the Acts of the Apostles? During those sermons he keeps on saying things like: *'The God of our fathers has raised up Jesus, whom you put to death.' (Acts 5:30)* and again, *'Whom God has raised up'* (Acts 2:22).

Doesn't that leave it open? There are two answers to this: one, that St Peter, inspired by the Holy Spirit, acting as Our Lord himself did during his public life, did not go around announcing that Jesus was the Messiah and indeed, God himself, the reason being that the Jews were not ready for this great revelation yet; it was enough for them to accept that they had put the Messiah to death not God himself; and the second reason is the explanation given by St Thomas Aquinas:

> *'One and the same power and operation belongs to the Father and the Son, hence both statements are true: Christ was raised by the divine power of the Father and his own; moreover, Christ sought and merited by prayer his Resurrection, that is as man, not as God.'*

Furthermore, we might add, do we not remember that Our Lord himself said, that <u>He would rise again</u> on the third day?

But the most important thing to remember is one of the phrases used as an Acclamation after the Consecration in the Holy Mass, where it says: '*dying you destroyed our death, rising you restored our life*'. The Redemption is incomplete unless we include the Resurrection.

And the reason for that is our need to rise again. One thing is for our sins to be forgiven and the other is for us to receive once more the sanctifying grace which was lost for us by our first parents. I said these two priests who said the death on the cross meant we were redeemed already and had no need for the resurrection, that it did not matter if Our Lord had risen or not. And the consequence of that is that we have lost the most important proof of his divinity. That is why, when it is suggested that the body or remains of Christ have been found some prominent Protestant theologians say it does not matter. Whether or not Our Lord rose from the dead or not is a matter of indifference. So, likewise, if told by the Moslems they have Our Lord's grave they remain unconcerned.

In addition to this we have what Fr Pope O.P. says in the notes to his edition of the New Testament: '*The Resurrection was a fact of so stupendous a nature that those who accepted it simply had to believe all that the Risen Christ claimed and taught. It is this that makes Christ's resurrection the cardinal fact to which the Apostles were especially called to bear witness cf. Acts 4:23 'Great was the power with which the apostles testified to the resurrection of Our Lord Jesus Christ' When you look into it, all the mysteries of Christianity take their origin from or have their explanation in the Resurrection of the Lord. If Our Lord had not risen our faith would be meaningless:*

> 'It is to heaven we look expectantly for the coming of Our Lord Jesus Christ to save us; he will form this humbled body of ours anew, moulding it into the image of his glorified body, so effective is his power to make all things obey him' (Phil 3:20-21).

Without the Resurrection, what would become of us? Our resurrection is spiritual in Jesus Christ:

> 'You know well enough that we who were taken up into Christ by Baptism have been taken up, all of us, into his Death. In our Baptism, we have been buried with him, died like him, that so, just as Christ was raised by his Father's power from the dead, we too might live and move in a new kind of existence' (Rom 6: 3-4).

In all of this, we should pause and consider how this affects us personally in a spiritual way. I find St Paul's words to the Colossians very appropriate:

> 'Risen, then, with Christ, you must lift your thoughts above, where Christ now sits at the right hand of God. You must be heavenly-minded, not earthly-minded; you have undergone death, and your life is hidden away now with Christ in God' (Col 3:1).

Baptism has placed in us the seed of grace, the seed of re-generation, and it will blossom forth, if we cultivate it with a deep interior life. Don't let us cast it aside through sin! Once we are solidly convinced of Our Lord's Resurrection and glorious Ascension into Heaven, our thoughts are elevated heavenwards. Where our thoughts tend so will our whole life. It is for this reason the liturgists insist that any authentic anaphora or Eucharistic prayer should have the anamnesis or remembrance of Our Lord's great work for our redemption which includes his Death, Resurrection and Ascension into Heaven. Some people forget that Our Lord instituted the Holy Eucharist as a great act of thanksgiving for us to make for his having redeemed us.

As we may remember, Pope Pius XII said the most pleasing prayer to God was thanksgiving. Furthermore, as it says in the Pastoral Constitution, *Gaudium et Spes*, n.22:

> 'Christ is risen, destroying death by his death. He has lavished life upon us, so that as sons in the Son, we can cry out in the Spirit: Abba, Father.'

This is telling us how, because of Christ's glorious Resurrection we have been made into children of God, able to look forward to our own resurrection and to tell others that they too can share in the fruits of Our Lord's Resurrection and so become saints wherever they are, no matter what condition of life they are in. We can repeat with St Josemaría that all the paths of the earth have been opened up, made divine, and so lead us to God and the happiness of Heaven.

THE ASCENSION OF OUR LORD AND THE COMING OF THE HOLY SPIRIT

OUR LORD IN HIS RISEN state stayed with his disciples, and they must have felt they were in Heaven. But it could not last. The reason he had chosen them was to continue his work; or now they were his Church. I have already explained, Christ chose to redeem us by entering the predicamental condition by taking on our human nature, so that, on the one hand he could suffer, and on the other, set us an example, to follow, this had, so-to-speak, the unfortunate consequence, that he had to live at a particular moment in history, live in a particular part of the world, and so could not reach every person himself, but only through persons imbued with his spirit and fired with his burning love.

Our Lord, then, ascended into Heaven, which had the immediate consequence that it was now up to the disciples to carry on where he had left off. But how are they to act in his stead? Our Lady shows them the way and we see described in the Acts of the Apostles how she took them back to the Cenacle and helped them to pray and prepare for the coming of the Holy Spirit. I cannot here just insert all the words of the Acts of the Apostles, but you can have the words to hand, and/or recall, how the Spirit came upon them as flaming tongues of fire that rested upon each one. There are several aspects of this which need our attention. The most important aspect is that the fire came in parted tongues, and came to rest on each one - this is telling us that the Holy Spirit acts on each individual soul. There are two points in *The Way* that bear this out. Firstly, we have no. 57:

> '*Get to know the Holy Spirit – the Great Unknown – for it is he who is to sanctify you*'.

The great pool of graces won by Our Lord with his sacrifice on the Cross, is available to all. But the graces have to be applied to the soul of each one. This is the work of the Holy Spirit, and he, therefore, is waiting for our own individual correspondence. '*Don't forget that you are God's temple. The Paraclete is in the centre of your soul: listen to him and be docile to his inspirations*'

Now the operative word here is *docility*, which is emphasised in St Josemaría's homily in '*Christ is Passing By*', entitled '*The Great Unknown*'. Docility involves both listening and then obeying. This is expressed in another point in *The Way*, no. 58:

> '*Don't hinder the work of the Paraclete: unite yourself to Christ, so as to be purified, and feel, with Him, the insults, and the spitting, and the blows..., and the thorns, and the weight of the cross..., and the iron nails tearing your flesh, and the anguish of a forsaken death...*
>
> *And enter into Our Lord Jesus' open side until you find sure refuge in his wounded Heart*'

Somewhere about 1932 I think it was, St Josemaría composed a beautiful prayer to the Holy Spirit which also expresses this notion of docility:

> '*Come, Oh Holy Spirit! Enlighten my understanding in order to know your commands; strengthen my heart against the snares of the enemy; enkindle my will. I have heard your voice, and I do not want to harden my heart and resist, saying, Later, tomorrow. Nunc coepi! now! Lest there be no tomorrow for me. Oh, Spirit of truth and of wisdom, Spirit of understanding and counsel, Spirit of joy and of peace: I want whatever you want; I want because you want; I want as you want; I want whenever you want.*'

Other teachers of the spiritual life also give us advice. Both Cardinal Manning and Blessed Abbot Marmion say something similar. In one of his books on the Holy Spirit, Cardinal Manning gives us words of warning

> *'Let us resolve, from this time, all we can, to love the Spirit of God, to conform ourselves to His will, worship Him day by day, to pray to Him personally, to place ourselves under His guidance, to beware of disobedience -of those three degrees of disobedience of which He Himself has warned us: Grieve not the Spirit of God, whereby ye are sealed unto the day of redemption (Eph 4:30), Resist not the Spirit (Acts 7: 51), Quench not the Spirit (I Thess 5: 19).*
>
> *These are the three degrees by which we may fall from His love and His presence.*
>
> *Beware also not of actual disobedience only, but of that tardy, slothful negligence by which you may provoke Him to a just impatience: 'Behold thou art neither cold nor hot, but lukewarm. I would thou wert either cold or hot.' Nothing provokes the Holy Spirit of God, who is the fire of the love of God than the lukewarmness with which we allow His graces and mercies to pass by us and pass by us unperceived.'*

Abbot Marmion expresses similar thoughts but in a different way:

> *'He makes His abode in our hearts that He may help and strengthen us; He will leave us only if we have the misfortune to drive Him from our souls by mortal sin.*
>
> *To drive out this spirit of love, by preferring the creature to Him in an absolute manner is what St Paul calls 'to quench the Spirit'. Moreover, let us follow the Apostle's counsel and not 'grieve' the Spirit; do not let us resist his inspirations, by any fully deliberate fault, however slight, by wilfully replying 'no' to the good He suggests to us. His action is extremely delicate, and*

> *when the soul resists Him deliberately and frequently, she forces Him little by little to be silent; then she comes to a standstill in the path of holiness, and even incurs great risk of leaving The Way of salvation, what can such a soul do, without a master to guide her, without light to enlighten her, without strength to sustain her, without joy to transport her?'*

These last few lines are remarkably similar to words of Francisca Javiera del Valle in her book on the Holy Spirit where she speaks of the Holy Spirit setting up his school in the centre of our soul and that if we do not put his advice into practice the school is shut and all the poor soul can do is to stay outside beg Him to open it once more.

THE GIFTS OF THE HOLY SPIRIT

Just as the virtues in the Christian life enable the will of man to obey more easily and sweetly right reason, so the gifts of the Holy Spirit enable man to follow the promptings and inspirations of the Holy Spirit. There are seven gifts all told, four which reside in the intellect: knowledge, understanding, wisdom and counsel, and three which reside in the will: piety, fortitude and the fear of the Lord. Overall, the work of the Holy Spirit is to acclimatise the soul to the supernatural world of God. By ourselves, following our human nature we are not really familiar with God's world, for by nature we belong to this world. There is nothing wrong with that but the purpose of life on earth is to prepare ourselves to live with God as citizens of heaven along with the Angels. This is the general work of the Holy Spirit to enable us to live in the supernatural world of God. He will give us the ability to think and act in a supernatural manner. Our Lord Jesus, because he was God, knew his way around the heavenly places, we, on the other hand do not naturally know our way, so the Holy Spirit familiarises us with God's world. The gifts, each in their own way, contribute their peculiar gift in this process. So, for example, the gift of understanding helps us grasp better the supernatural truths by which God lives, the gift of knowledge helps us appreciate the heavenly values as opposed to the earthly works and achievements. Wisdom enhances in us the virtue of charity so that we are enabled to direct all our human actions towards God and whatever he loves. The gift of counsel equipped with the other gifts enables the soul to enlighten and guide others to their supernatural destiny. Very often we find in life there is a deep-seated yearning or longing for earthly pleasures and satisfactions. Many souls become totally enslaved by human passions in this way. What the gift of fear of God does is to quench this longing and replace it with a longing and deep-seated desire of satisfying God's will that we should love him. We remember how in the Gospel, Our Lord said to his disciples they must either love God or mammon and could not love both.

Well, the gift of fear - setting aside the servile fear which just tries to please God so one will not be punished - fills the soul with a wonderful, uplifting longing to give pleasure to God in his great longing that we should love him, setting aside the sickly earthly desire to satisfy our passions. The gift of piety is similarly set on satisfying God's great love for us, helping us to live our spirit of divine filiation, so that the soul is all the time wanting to be a true and loving son of God. And in our life and behaviour as the sons of God, the gift of fortitude enables us to have the strength to follow God's plan in all its detail, never hesitating or wavering when God's glory is at stake.

As a consequence of our response to the promptings of the Holy Spirit through our possession of his wonderful gifts, each soul reflects the consequences of this supernatural way of living with the fruits of the Holy Spirit. I think St Paul lists twelve fruits. There are, in fact, many more. The eight beatitudes are all fruits of the Holy Spirit and other wonderful manifestations of the salutary effect of the Holy Spirit in those souls privileged to receive his Gifts. These are amply demonstrated in the lives of the holy Apostles which we see described in the Acts of the Apostles, and which are seen in the history of the whole Church in the lives of the Saints.

Printed and bound by CPI Group (UK) Ltd, Croydon, CR0 4YY